Historical American Biographies

ABIGAIL ADAMS

First Lady and Patriot

Pat McCarthy

Enslow Publishers, Inc.

40 Industrial Road   PO Box 38
Box 398   Aldershot
Berkeley Heights, NJ 07922   Hants GU12 6BP
USA   UK

http://www.enslow.com

To my sister, Kay Reall, who always supports me in everything I do.

Library of Congress Cataloging-in-Publication Data

McCarthy, Pat.
    Abigail Adams : First Lady and patriot / Pat McCarthy.
        p. cm. — (Historical American biographies)
    Includes bibliographical references (p.) and index.
    ISBN 0-7660-1618-8
    1. Adams, Abigail, 1744–1818—Juvenile literature. 2. Adams, John, 1735–1826—Juvenile literature. 3. Presidents's spouses—United States—Biography—Juvenile literature. [1. Adams, Abigail, 1744–1818. 2. First ladies. 3. Women—Biography.] I. Title. II. Series.
    E322.1.A38 M37   2002
    973.4'4'092—dc21
                                            2001000709

Printed in the United States of America

10 9 8 7 6 5 4 3 2 1

To Our Readers: We have done our best to make sure all Internet addresses in this book were active and appropriate when we went to press. However, the author and the publisher have no control over and assume no liability for the material available on those Internet sites or on other Web sites they may link to. Any comments or suggestions can be sent by e-mail to comments@enslow.com or to the address on the back cover.

Illustration Credits: Adams National Historic Site, pp. 46, 56, 85, 92, 99; Enslow Publishers, Inc., pp. 11, 25; Reproduced from the *Dictionary of American Portraits*, Published by Dover Publications, Inc., in 1967, pp. 4, 22, 35, 39, 50, 64, 79, 87, 103, 114; Library of Congress, pp. 6, 15, 66, 70, 83; John Grafton, Grafton, *Pictorial Sourcebook of Copyright Free Graphics*, 1974 Dover Publications, NY, pp. 28, 31, 42, 76.

Cover Illustration: Portrait of Abigail Adams, *U.S. Dept. of the Interior, National Park Service, Adams National Historical Park.* Background: Battle of Bunker Hill, *National Archives.*

CONTENTS

Abigail and John Adams

1

A WAR BEGINS

The sounds of distant gunfire woke Abigail Adams and her four children before dawn on June 17, 1775. All through the hot morning, they heard the dull boom of cannons. Finally, Abigail and her seven-year-old son, John Quincy, climbed to the top of Penn's Hill, across from their home in Braintree, Massachusetts.[1]

Through the smoke, they saw the ruins of Charlestown, across the bay, which the British had just set afire. They watched in horror as British soldiers, called redcoats, swarmed up nearby Breed's Hill. The acrid smell of gunpowder filled the air. Another battle in the Revolutionary War had begun.

The colonial army had worked all night fortifying Breed's Hill, hoping they could win Boston back from the British. The British had occupied the city for nearly two months. The battle, known as the Battle of Bunker Hill, was mostly fought on nearby Breed's Hill.

To save precious ammunition, Colonel William Prescott, who commanded the colonial army in the battle, is supposed to have ordered, "Don't shoot till you see the whites of their eyes."[2] As British troops marched up the hill, they wondered why the colonists were not firing. At last, the order came, and a tremendous volley of shots mowed down hundreds of redcoats. The British retreated. Twice more they tried to advance. The third time they were victorious. The colonists had run out of ammunition. Still, they continued to fight, using their rifles as clubs.

In June 1775, Abigail Adams and her son, John Quincy, witnessed the burning of Charlestown, Massachusetts, by British troops, one of the violent confrontations of the American Revolution.

The British won the battle but suffered tremendous losses. There were more than a thousand British casualties. More than one hundred patriots died in the battle.

Soon Abigail Adams got disturbing news. Joseph Warren, a handsome young doctor and a good friend of the family, had died in the battle. Warren was a leader of the patriots, those who were loyal to the colonies. He held the rank of general but had chosen to fight under Prescott in the battle.

It was Warren who had alerted Paul Revere two months ago, on April 18, 1775. Revere was to warn Abigail's husband, John Adams, and his friend John Hancock that the British were coming to Boston. The colonists feared an attack.

Abigail Adams wrote to her husband, John, "My bursting Heart must find vent at my pen. I have just heard that our dear Friend Dr. Warren is no more but fell gloriously fighting for his Country . . . Great is our Loss."[3]

Soon after the Battle of Bunker Hill, seven-year-old Johnny saw his mother and Uncle Elihu Adams putting her precious pewter spoons into a large kettle. He realized they were melting them down to make bullets. Sixty-eight years later, he asked, "Do you wonder that a boy of seven years who witnessed this scene should be a patriot?"[4]

The Second Continental Congress, made up of representatives from all the colonies, was set to meet in Philadelphia on May 10 to plan united action. John Adams was a delegate.

"The die is cast," he told his wife. "My Lord Mansfield has said in Parliament [British legislature] that if we do not defend ourselves, they will kill us. We will defend ourselves."[5]

The Beginning of the American Revolution

The American Revolution had begun on April 19, 1775, when British soldiers marched on Lexington, to confiscate American ammunition in nearby Concord, Massachusetts. The colonial minutemen (soldiers who claimed to be ready to fight at a minute's notice) were waiting. Eight Americans died in the battle.

Then the British marched to Concord, where they intended to seize the ammunition and start back to Boston. More than three hundred minutemen were lying in wait at a bridge outside Concord. Two more Americans and three British soldiers were killed in the exchange of shots. As the British marched back to Boston, colonists continued to fire at them from behind trees, rocks, and fences. By the time they reached the city, seventy British soldiers were dead and twice that many injured.

This was the first of many long separations for the Adams family. While John Adams was busy helping to chart the course of history, Abigail Adams was left with four small children on the little farm in Braintree.

As always, Abigail rose to the occasion. She would manage the house and farm and take care of the children. She proved herself to be an extraordinary woman.

2

THE PREACHER'S DAUGHTER GROWS UP

A bigail Smith was born in Weymouth, Massachusetts, on November 22, 1744, to Reverend William Smith and Elizabeth Quincy Smith. Her older sister, Mary, was three.

William Smith's father had been a well-to-do merchant in Boston, but young William went to Harvard where he prepared to become a minister. He married Elizabeth Quincy, whose father, John, was the leading citizen of nearby Braintree. Quincy was a descendant of one of the signers of the Magna Carta.[1]

Reverend Smith was well liked in his parish and was respected by the community. John Adams noted in his diary that Smith was a good judge of people. His ability to understand their feelings made him a successful minister.[2]

The Magna Carta

The Magna Carta was a document agreed to by King John of England in 1215. It guaranteed English people certain rights. These included the right to own property, to have justice, and not to have taxes levied without consent. It laid the foundation for the democratic governments, including that of the United States, that would come in the future.

Abigail as a Small Child

Little Abigail was a frail, dark-haired child with fair skin and wide-set dark eyes.[3] Throughout her childhood, she always seemed to be sick. She was shy and reserved, but her mother worried about her stubborn streak. Grandmother Elizabeth Quincy reassured her daughter, "Wild colts make the best horses."[4]

Abigail's father taught her "to say all the handsome things she could of Persons but not Evil—and to make Things rather than Persons the Subjects of Conversations."[5] Abigail liked to help him with the chores, and when she was ten, he gave her a pet lamb.[6]

Elizabeth was a devoted mother and minister's wife. She treated everyone in the parish kindly and stayed out of disagreements. She helped the sick and unfortunate and taught her girls to do the same. "We should never wait to be requested to do a kind office, an act of love," she told them.[7] Abigail often went with her when she visited people.

Elizabeth Quincy Smith taught her girls to cook, sew, clean, raise vegetables and chickens, and nurse the sick. They had to do chores even though the family had servants.

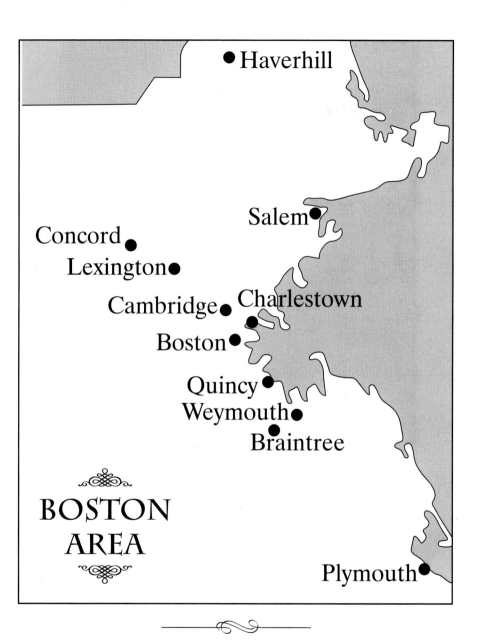

BOSTON AREA

Haverhill

Concord
Lexington
Cambridge   Charlestown
Boston
Quincy
Weymouth
Braintree

Salem

Plymouth

John Adams often traveled from their home in Braintree to do legal work in bigger cities, such as Boston.

The Smith girls knew their roles as adults would be as wives and mothers, like most women of their time.

Weymouth was a pleasant seaside town about ten miles south of Boston. A dirt road led north through Braintree to Boston, and it was necessary to cross rivers and streams with no bridges. People walked, or traveled on horseback, or in a chaise, a little wagon pulled by a horse.

Education

Abigail liked to visit her Quincy grandparents. The little girl loved to stay at Mount Wollaston, their large estate. Tall, white-haired Grandfather Quincy shared his extensive library with her, and Abigail considered her grandmother her first and best teacher. Abigail later wrote to her own daughter, Nabby,

> I have not forgotten the excellent lessons which I received from my grandmother, at a very early period of life. . . . Whether it was owing to the happy method of mixing instruction and amusement together . . . I know not. . . . I love and revere her memory; her lively, cheerful disposition animated all around her.[8]

Abigail never attended school. Girls had to be able to read the Bible and perform basic math but they were not expected to learn much beyond that. The Smiths were different. Abigail's mother taught her to read at an early age, and she studied French, then her father took over her education. There were few schools for girls at the time, and Elizabeth Smith worried about illnesses, so she preferred to teach her girls at home. Abigail inherited her father's love of reading and was determined to educate herself. As an adult, she felt her schooling had been deficient, even though she was one of the best-read women of her time.

Visits to Boston

During her teen years, Abigail often visited her aunt and uncle, Isaac and Elizabeth Smith, in Boston. Uncle Isaac was a wealthy merchant and shipowner. Aunt Elizabeth was not as protective as Abigail's mother. Abigail shared books belonging to her cousin Isaac, who, although five years younger, was already preparing for Harvard.

Here, Abigail made friends her own age. Being in Boston was a refreshing change from the sleepy town of Weymouth. She liked the faster pace of life there. She and her friends enjoyed watching the ships in the harbor. They loved to see the latest fashions from London and to walk along the maze of narrow, crooked cobblestone streets.

Writing Letters

Abigail kept in touch with her Boston friends through letter writing. Their letters were designed to "improve their minds and polish their writing styles."[9] One of her correspondents was Hannah Storer, Aunt Elizabeth's younger sister. Hannah was six years older than Abigail but became a close friend. Writers of the time often used classical pen names. Abigail called herself Diana, after the Roman goddess of the moon.

In her teens, Abigail began to worry about finding a husband. As a shy, insecure teenager, she felt no man would ever want to marry her. Hannah, newly married, invited her to visit. Abigail wrote back, "You bid me tell *one* of my sparks [boyfriends] to bring me to see you. Why! I believe you think they are as plenty as herrings, when, alas! there is as great a scarcity of them as there is of justice, honesty, prudence, and many other virtues. I've no pretensions to one."[10]

Abigail soon changed her mind when a young lawyer named John Adams showed an interest in her.

3

LOVE AND MARRIAGE

W hen she was fifteen, Abigail Smith met John
Adams. The twenty-four-year-old lawyer's first
impression of the Smith girls was not flattering. In his
diary, he admitted that they were "wits" but considered
them to be lacking in tenderness.[1] For their part, the girls
thought Adams talked too much.

Two years later, John Adams changed his mind about
Abigail. Adams often came to visit the Smiths with his
friend Richard Cranch. Cranch was tall, handsome, and
charming. John Adams, on the other hand, was short and a
little overweight, with a round, chubby face. He also
tended to be rather blunt.[2]

Cranch was courting Abigail's older sister, Mary, but he
took Abigail's passion for learning seriously. He helped her
study French, let her borrow books, and introduced her to

Abigail fell in love with John Adams, a promising young attorney, seen here in later years.

contemporary English literature. Abigail always held Cranch in a special place in her heart.

A Passionate Romance

In time, John Adams and Abigail discovered that they were strongly attracted to each other. This attraction would last for the rest of their lives. They had trouble keeping their passion under control, but as a minister's daughter, Abigail knew it was important to be discreet.

Abigail's father was the only family member who appreciated John's finer qualities. Her mother did not think his family background was prestigious enough, and she did not want Abigail to marry a lawyer. In the colonies, lawyers were often looked down on.

John Adams came from a good family, but it did not have the high social standing the Smiths and Quincys enjoyed. John's father, a farmer, urged him to go to college. John graduated from Harvard, then studied law. There were few lawyers in the area, and he was very serious about his work. In time, Abigail's family came to accept him.

At first, Abigail was a little shy with John. She was intimidated by his bold and forthright manner. Soon, however, she felt more at ease and realized they had much in common. An entry in John's diary when Abigail was eighteen years old showed how much his feelings had changed from his first impression: "Tender feelings, sensible, friendly. A friend. Not an imprudent, not an indelicate or a disagreeable Word or Action. Prudent, modest, delicate, soft, sensible, obliging, active."[3] He had come to appreciate Abigail's wit and intelligence.

John Adams was sensitive and understanding and was not afraid to express his feelings. His sense of humor was similar to Abigail's, and he encouraged her interest in books.

The two were soon discussing marriage. John had inherited a house and farm and could afford to marry. Abigail was eighteen, however, and her parents considered her too young to marry.

Courtship

John rode the circuit, arguing cases in different area courts. Whenever he was gone, the two exchanged long love letters. They addressed each other by their pen names, Diana and Lysander (a Spartan military commander). John sometimes started his letters, "Miss Adorable."[4] Their letters were teasing and tender and expressed their deepest feelings.

In one letter, Abigail told John she thought he was too severe in his judgments of people. She then asked him to list her faults.

He responded with a detailed list: She did not play cards well, did not blush easily enough, had never learned to sing, sometimes hung her head, crossed her legs, and walked with her toes pointing in.[5]

Her response was quick. She said, "I thank you for your Catalogue, but must confess I was so hardened as to read over most of my Faults with as much pleasure, as an other person would have read their perfections."[6] She said she neglected singing because she had "a voice harsh as the screech of a peacock."[7] And she wrote, "The fifth fault, will endeavour to amend of it, but you know I think that a gentleman has no business to concern himself about the Leggs of a Lady."[8]

They had hoped to marry in the spring of 1764, but an outbreak of smallpox postponed their plans. John decided to be inoculated against the disease, since his work brought

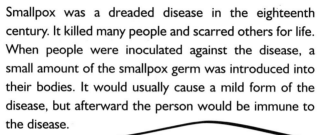

Inoculation

Smallpox was a dreaded disease in the eighteenth century. It killed many people and scarred others for life. When people were inoculated against the disease, a small amount of the smallpox germ was introduced into their bodies. It would usually cause a mild form of the disease, but afterward the person would be immune to the disease.

him in contact with many people. His brother, Peter, would be inoculated with him.

A Postponed Engagement

John would remain in Boston at least six weeks. Abigail wanted to be inoculated, too, but her mother considered it too dangerous and would not allow it.

The time apart was hard for them both. Hoping to kill the germs that caused smallpox, John had his letters smoked before he sent them. When the letters arrived, they were smoked again, just to be sure.

John described the inoculation:

> Dr. Perkins demanded my left Arm and Dr. Warren my Brothers. They took their Launcetts [knives] and with their Points divided the skin for about a quarter of an Inch and just suffering the Blood to appear, buried a Thread about a Quarter inch long in the Channell. A little Lint was then laid over the scratch and a Piece of Ragg pressed on, and then a Bandage bound over all.[9]

He boasted that he passed the smallpox with "fewer Pains, Achs, and Qualms" than anyone he had known. "I had no Pain in my Back, none in my side, none in my Head.

None in my Bones or Limbs, no retching or vomiting or sickness. A short shivering Fit, and a succeeding hot glowing Fit, a Want of Appetite, and a general Languor, were all the symptoms . . . that I can Boast of."[10]

In May 1764, he returned, and they began wedding preparations. Abigail went to Boston for a brief visit with her aunt and uncle and promptly got sick. John had to hire the household help and furnish his house, which was next door to his mother's.

In the midst of his preparations, he went to Plymouth for a circuit court session. He wrote, "Oh my dear Girl, I thank Heaven that another Fortnight [two weeks] will restore you to me—after so long a separation."[11]

John and Abigail were married in Weymouth on October 25, 1764, with Abigail's father presiding as minister. She would be twenty the next month. Her new husband was twenty-nine.

After the ceremony, the new Mr. and Mrs. Adams went to a small house on the farm. There, they would spend many years of their married life.

4

UNREST IN THE COLONIES

The Adamses' first year of marriage was carefree and happy. The newlyweds took long walks and climbed nearby Penn's Hill. On a clear day, they could see all the way to Boston, ten miles away. Sleigh rides livened up the cold winter days, and they spent most evenings reading by the fireside.

They raised chickens, vegetables, and fruit and had cows and sheep. Braintree had no stores, so they went to Boston to buy such necessities as fish, meat, flour, sugar, and tea.

When she was not working in the garden, Abigail Adams spent much of her time in the big kitchen with the huge fireplace. She cooked over an open fire, using heavy cast-iron pots. The oven, heated by coals, was a hollowed-out area in the side of the fireplace. She made most of their clothes from fabrics she ordered from Boston. She knew how to spin and weave, but the cloth was coarse and plain. Although she had a servant, Abigail did much of the work herself.

John Adams loved working the land, but his law practice was growing rapidly. The traveling lifestyle of a lawyer was often hard on the newlyweds. Their first separation came three months after the wedding, when he had to attend a court session in Boston.

Starting a Family

Abigail Adams had become pregnant almost immediately after the wedding. She and John were both excited to be starting a family of their own. When the baby came, John was away at court.

Baby Abigail, called Nabby, was born on July 14, 1765. Abigail's mother and sisters were with her for the delivery and helped her for three weeks while she regained her strength.

Abigail wrote happily to her friend Hannah in Boston, saying, "Your Diana become a Mamma—can you credit it?" She said Nabby's "pretty smiles already delight my Heart, who is the Dear Image of her still Dearer Pappa."[1]

War Brewing

Their peaceful family life soon ended. There was increasing unrest in the American colonies. British King George III and British Minister George Grenville thought that since the British government had to cover the expense of governing and protecting the colonies, the colonies should generate some income for England. On March 24, Parliament passed the Stamp Act. Stamps had to be affixed to all legal documents such as marriage licenses, diplomas, and leases to show the tax had been paid. Stamps were required even on

Samuel Adams, John's cousin, was one of the foremost patriots in the years leading up to the American Revolution.

newspapers, pamphlets, and playing cards.

The colonists, especially those in Boston, protested violently. "There is no room for delay," advised Samuel Adams, John's cousin. "These unexpected proceedings may be preparatory to more extensive taxation."[2]

John Adams agreed that the Stamp Act was both illegal and unconstitutional, since the colonists had no representatives in Parliament. Abigail, who always had political opinions of her own, agreed. Massachusetts judges refused to use stamps on court documents. As punishment for disobeying the law, Parliament closed the courts in the colony.

With no legal business to transact, John began editing and writing articles for the *Boston Gazette*, giving his point of view on the crisis. He acknowledged his loyalty to the king but said, "We can never be slaves."[3] He quickly became a major spokesman for the colonies.

The Stamp Act was repealed in March 1766. By now, John had become a well-known political figure, as well as a busy lawyer.

Family Reunions

Mary and Richard Cranch, who had been married more than three years, moved to Salem. It was the first time the two sisters had been separated. So in August 1766, John took Abigail to Salem for a visit with her sister. They traveled in an open chaise, and the twenty-five-mile trip took two days. When their visit ended, it was hard to leave. Abigail wanted Nabby and Betsey, Mary's daughter, to grow up together. She said she would give a lot to "see them put their little arms around one an others necks, and hug each other."[4]

In the fall, John and Abigail Adams visited the Cranches again. During the trip, both Adamses had their portraits painted by a local artist named Benjamin Blyth. The painter caught Abigail with the hint of a smile, making her appear thoughtful and reserved. Her dark hair was pulled back with a bow. She looked fashionable in her low-necked dress, set off by three strands of pearls. In his portrait, John looked younger than he was, with his plump face and pink cheeks.

Abigail's Readings

Abigail Adams read a lot. One of her favorite authors was Reverend James Fordyce, an English minister. His books stressed the importance of feminine modesty. He said women were made to be helpmates for their husbands. But he urged young women to make the most of their intelligence by reading extensively. He thought they had the ability to influence the world through their children.[5]

Another Addition to the Family

On July 11, 1767, Abigail gave birth to another baby. John Quincy Adams was named for Abigail's grandfather, who died two days later. While John was at court, she wrote and told him Nabby had rocked the baby in his cradle, singing, "Come pappa come home to Brother Johnny."[6]

Abigail took most of the responsibility of raising the children. Nabby's and John Quincy's health was her biggest concern. Due to diseases and lack of modern medicine, many children of the time died before their second birthday.

With much of his work going on in Boston, John Adams decided to move the family there. In April 1768, they moved into a rented house on Brattle Square, in the middle of the city.

Abigail had always loved Boston. Sixteen thousand people lived in the lively, crowded city. The clop-clop of horses' hooves and the clatter of wagons sounded late into the night.

Abigail enjoyed being close to friends and family, including her sister Mary, who had recently moved there. She loved reading the weekly newspapers as soon as they came off the press. Sometimes she agreed with what she read, and sometimes she did not, but she always had an opinion.

A few months later, British troops arrived in Boston. The British believed they could quiet the Massachusetts radicals before their ideas spread to other colonies. The soldiers chose Brattle Square for their daily drills, so Abigail and the children heard the thud of marching feet all day.

A Tragic Loss

A third child, Susanna, was born on December 28. She was named for John's mother. Little Suky, as Susanna was called, was sickly from the start. Abigail spent months trying herbal remedies and rocking the baby to sleep at night, but Suky died on February 4, 1770. She was just thirteen months old. Abigail was devastated. She would not even talk or write about the tragedy.

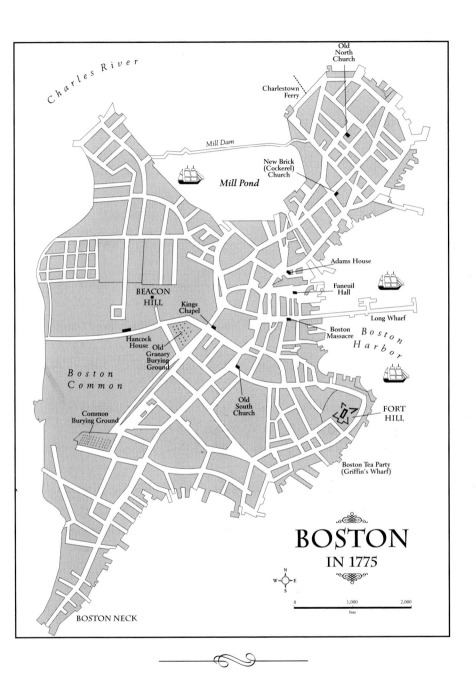

Abigail Adams loved living in Boston, which was brimming with patriot activity at the time the Adamses moved there.

John spent many evenings talking politics with patriot leaders. Although he felt guilty about neglecting his family, he felt a duty to public service.

The Adamses had moved into a house on Cold Lane, and friends were always welcome. Frequent visitors included Sam Adams, John Hancock, and Abigail's cousin, Josiah Quincy. Their doctor, Joseph Warren, was also a great favorite. Abigail sat in on political discussions. She did not usually say much, since it was considered improper for women of the time to have political opinions. However, she and John discussed everything afterward.

The men were irate about the Townshend Acts, which placed a tax on lead, glass, paper, paint, and tea shipped into the colonies from England. They decided to boycott, or refuse to buy, all British products. Sam Adams, who was already entertaining ideas of American independence from Great Britain, formed a secret organization called the Sons of Liberty.

In response to the boycott, Abigail and other women started weaving their own cloth and serving coffee instead of tea. They also made tea from leaves, berries, and herbs. These homemade brews came to be known as liberty teas.

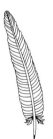

A Trip to England?

When Abigail learned that her cousin Isaac Smith, Jr., was going to make a trip to England, she wrote to him, saying, "From my infancy I have always felt a great inclination to visit the Mother Country, . . . and had nature formed me of the other Sex, I should certainly have been a rover."[7]

The Boston Massacre

On the night of March 5, 1770, Abigail was at home with the children. John was attending a meeting. About 9:00 P.M., gunshots rang out and bells clanged. The men rushed out of the meeting, thinking there was a fire. John rushed home. Abigail was pregnant, and he feared she would run out into the icy streets to see what was happening. He hurried past the soldiers, hoping they would ignore him. The Adamses soon learned that British soldiers had shot several Bostonians. Three were dead, two were mortally injured, and several others were hurt.

The scuffle, known as the Boston Massacre, had broken out after gangs of young men had taunted the British soldiers, shouting names such as "Lobsters!" and "Bloody Backs!" and throwing snowballs, sticks, and oyster shells. Someone in the crowd yelled "Fire!" and the soldiers let go with a volley of shots into the crowd.

British Captain Thomas Preston and several soldiers were arrested. John agreed to defend them. He realized he might ruin his reputation as a patriot, but he did not hesitate. He believed in the right of an accused person to legal counsel, and he thought that if the soldiers got a fair trial, the British would see that Bostonians believed in justice. He and Abigail discussed the issue far into the night. She agreed with his decision to take the case.

While preparing his case, John was elected to the Massachusetts legislature. Through a flood of tears at the thought of separation, Abigail told him he had to accept. She said she was "very willing to share in all that was to come."[8]

During the trial, Captain Preston was acquitted of wrongdoing. So were six of the soldiers. The other two

Paul Revere made this engraving of the Boston Massacre, in which British soldiers fired into a crowd of local people. John Adams would be the lawyer who defended the British soldiers when they went to court for their actions.

were convicted of manslaughter, which means killing another person without bad intentions. As punishment, they were branded on their thumbs and released. Aside from a few rumors that John Adams was a Tory (loyal to the British king), his reputation was untarnished.

Back to the Country

Meanwhile, the Adams family was growing. That same summer, a second son, Charles, was born.

That winter, John experienced chest pains and a racking cough. He decided he needed fresh country air in order to recuperate, so the Adamses moved back to the farm. He kept his law office in Boston and commuted on horseback. He wrote in his diary, "Farewell politics!"[9]

For a year and a half, John did not participate in politics. Abigail was happy, with all of them together back on the farm. Fortunately, this period saw a lull in the conflict between Great Britain and the colonies, from 1771 to 1772. Otherwise, John probably could not have kept his promise.

John and Abigail both hated the times he had to be away from home, representing clients in regional courts. "I want to see my Wife and Children every Day," he wrote to her.[10]

By the fall of 1772, there was another little Adams. Thomas was born on September 15. Soon, the long commute from Braintree to Boston became too much for John, so the Adamses moved back to the city. They bought a large brick house on South Queen Street and moved in on November 24. The calm that they had enjoyed for a year and a half was about to end, and they would be right in the middle of the action.

The Rebellion Begins

The British had repealed the Townshend Acts in March 1770. Now only the tax on tea remained. Patriots thought the tea tax was being retained just to prove that Great Britain could tax the colonists. The patriots particularly resented the 1773 Tea Act, which gave a monopoly of the tea trade to the British East India Company. When three ships carrying tea arrived in Boston Harbor in December, the patriots would not allow them to be unloaded. Abigail wrote to a friend, "The Tea that bainful [harmful or poisonous] weed is arrived. Great and I hope Effectual opposition has been made to the landing of it."[11]

On Thursday evening, December 16, colonists held a meeting to make a final appeal to Governor Thomas Hutchinson to end the tax. Hutchinson refused, and confusion reigned. Then, a war whoop sounded, and a shout went up, "Boston harbor a teapot tonight."[12] As darkness fell, the Sons of Liberty, disguised as American Indians, crept on board the three ships that carried the controversial tea. They dumped 342 chests of tea into the water. John Adams wrote in his diary, "Last Night 3 Cargoes of Bohea Tea were emptied into the Sea . . . This is the most magnificent Movement of all . . . I cant but consider it as an Epocha in History."[13]

The British Parliament took drastic measures, closing Boston Harbor to all trade. British General Thomas Gage sailed into the harbor on May 13, 1774, to take over as Commander in Chief of British forces. The British were determined to subdue the Bostonians. Immediately, the colonists called a meeting of representatives from all colonies. The meeting, called the First Continental Congress, would be held in Philadelphia. According to

Most patriots hailed the Boston Tea Party, which helped unite the American colonies in their resistance to British rule.

John's diary, the Congress would "devise a plan for a more lasting accommodation with Great Britain."[14] John was a delegate. He and Abigail agreed that he had a duty to serve. They both dreaded war but now they thought it might be inevitable.

John left home on August 10. He and Abigail said their private good-byes. Then she stood in the street with the cheering crowds that had gathered to see the delegates off. She hated to be separated from John, but she was willing to stay home with the children while her husband went off to make history.

5

EARLY YEARS OF THE REVOLUTION

John Adams confided to James Warren that he felt inadequate to be a delegate to the Congress: "I am at a loss, totally at a loss, what to do when we get there."[1]

In John's absence, Abigail Adams took responsibility for running the farm in Braintree. She hired workers and made business decisions. John was proud of her and joked that the neighbors would think their business affairs ran more smoothly when he was gone.[2]

Teacher and Correspondent

Abigail also took charge of the education of their children. She was confident she could teach nine-year-old Nabby, since girls needed only to be able to read, write, and do a little arithmetic. She worried, however, about John Quincy. At seven, John Quincy should be going to school to learn Latin and Greek. Most schools were shut down because of the problems with England, so she asked John Thaxter, who had worked in John's law office, to tutor him. John Adams agreed with the decision. He wrote of his sons, "John has genius, and so does Charles. Take care that they don't go astray. Cultivate their minds, inspire their little hearts . . . Nabby . . . by reason of her sex, requires a different education from the two I have mentioned. Of this, you are the only judge."[3]

Abigail kept John up to date on happenings in the area. He, in turn, informed her of what was going on in Congress. At this time, most colonists were not thinking of independence from Great Britain. They still considered themselves British. They just wanted fair treatment and more say in the laws that governed them.

John was impatient with the lack of organization in the colonial army. One morning, John said to Sam Adams, "I am determined this morning to make a direct motion that Congress should adopt the army before Boston, and appoint Colonel [George] Washington commander of it."[4] John made the motion, and after some discussion, Washington was appointed commander. Congress then sent

George Washington

George Washington had been a member of the House of Burgesses, the Virginia colonial legislature. He was also a wealthy planter who owned slaves, and a member of the Anglican Church. His skill and experience as an officer in the French and Indian War made him a good choice as Commander in Chief of American forces during the Revolution.

George Washington was named Commander in Chief of the American forces, a decision both John and Abigail Adams believed was a good one.

ten companies of riflemen to Boston.

John wrote to Abigail, "I can now inform you that the Congress have made Choice of the modest and virtuous, the amiable, generous and brave George Washington Esqr., to be the General of the American Army, and that he is to repair as soon as possible to the Camp before Boston."[5]

When Washington arrived in Massachusetts, he called on Abigail Adams. She described him to John: "Dignity with ease, and complacency, the Gentleman and Soldier look agreeable blended in him. Modesty marks every line and feature of his face."[6]

Declaration of Rights and Grievances

The First Continental Congress issued the Declaration of Rights and Grievances in October 1774, a petition to King George III. Congress also called for the colonies to boycott trade with the British and set up Committees of Safety to enforce the boycott.

Congress adjourned on October 26, 1774, after planning to reassemble in Philadelphia on May 10, 1775, for a Second Continental Congress. John spent all winter at home. After the Battles of Lexington and Concord took place in April 1775, the American Revolution began. John Adams went back to Philadelphia to help his fellow patriots organize the war effort.

The British Army occupied Boston, and local people fled from the city, carrying with them anything they could. The British did not allow many of the people to leave at all.

Boston was only half an hour's ride from Braintree, so a daily stream of refugees passed by the Adams home. Abigail did her part to help, letting people stay for the night or sometimes even for a week. She wrote to John, "The house is a Scene of Confusion . . . you can hardly imagine how we live."[7]

Once she housed an entire company of militiamen on their way to Boston. They slept in the attic, in the barn, and on the parlor floor. The next morning, they drilled in the field behind the house. They were joined by little John Quincy, who marched up and down with them, pretending that he was a soldier, too.

When the Second Continental Congress recessed in August, John went to Watertown, a few miles west of Boston, to attend sessions of the Massachusetts General Court. Abigail did not mind his absence as terribly as usual, since he came home on weekends.

A Dangerous Epidemic

A major epidemic of dysentery, then often a fatal illness, raged in the area. Dysentery caused cramps, vomiting, fever, and diarrhea. While John was at Watertown, he received bad news from Abigail. "Your brother Elihu lies very dangerously sick with a Dysentery . . . his life is dispaired of . . . We are all in great distress. Your mother is with him in great anguish."[8] Elihu died the next day, leaving three orphaned children, since his wife had died earlier.

Abigail came down with dysentery; then three-year-old Thomas became extremely sick, and she got out of bed to take care of him. Abigail's mother came every day to help nurse her and little Thomas. Soon she, too, had the illness. Thomas had improved by now, but Patty, a servant girl, lay close to death.

Abigail, now feeling better, traveled back and forth from Braintree to Weymouth, caring for both her mother and Patty. She wrote about "the distress of my dear Mother. Her kindness brought her to see me every day when I was ill and our little Tommy. She has taken the disorder and lies so bad that we have little hopes of her Recovery. She is posses'd with the idea that she shall not recover, and I fear it will prove but too true."[9]

Elizabeth Smith's premonition was correct. On October 1, Abigail heard a gasp, and her mother looked at her with "a look that pierced my heart, and which I shall never forget! it was the eagerness of a last look."[10]

Brokenhearted, Abigail wrote to John in Philadelphia: "How can I tell you (o my bursting Heart) that my Dear Mother has Left me . . ."[11] John wished he could go home to comfort his wife, but he felt obligated to continue his work in Congress. He wrote special notes to the children, sympathizing with them on the loss of their grandmother.

The next week, Patty died, too, after lying ill for over a month. First Elihu, then her mother, and now Patty had all fallen victim to dysentery. Grief-stricken, Abigail did not visit anyone except her father and sisters for weeks. As a child and teenager, she had resented her mother's worries about her. Now a mother herself, she could understand her mother's feelings and wished that she had been more patient. She remembered her love, wit, and patience.

Abigail agreed to take in one of Elihu's little daughters. The presence of the little girl helped take her mind off her losses.

Although Congress had not adjourned, John came home for Christmas. He was able to stay for only a month, but their time together helped raise Abigail's spirits.

Progress of the War

The war hád been going badly for the colonies. The British soldiers were better equipped and better trained than the disorganized Americans. While John was home, General Washington and his troops crossed the Delaware River to Trenton and surprised the British there. They captured a thousand Hessians (German soldiers paid to fight for the British), plus arms and ammunition. This was the first encouraging news from the war front in a long time.

After he returned to Philadelphia, John sent Abigail a copy of Thomas Paine's pamphlet *Common Sense*. Paine argued that the colonies should declare themselves independent of Great Britain, rather than try to reconcile with the king. John and Abigail both agreed, although John did not agree with the form of government Paine proposed. Paine wanted a legislature with just one house, while John thought two houses were necessary.

In March, General Washington's men placed artillery on Dorchester Heights, overlooking Boston. From there, they could bombard the city, now held by the British, with shells. Realizing his situation, British General Thomas Gage evacuated Boston.

Over the last year, the British had realized that the rebellion was far more widespread than they had first believed. The activities of the Continental Congress convinced them that the rebellion was not limited to Boston.

New Friends, New Ideas

Like John, Abigail was becoming convinced that independence was the only choice for the American colonies. She
began corresponding with two women who held similar views.

Mercy Warren was the wife of John's friend James
Warren. Mercy was older—forty-five to Abigail's twenty-
nine—when they first met. Mercy Warren was active in the
American patriotic cause and had published a play called
The Adulateur in 1772. Acting was not permitted in
Boston, so her political plays were meant only to be read.

Abigail's other correspondent was Catharine Macaulay,
an Englishwoman. Macaulay was interested in American
women and wrote letters to both Mercy Warren and Abigail
Adams. She was a brilliant historian who backed the
American cause.

By March 1776, Abigail thought independence was
inevitable, and her thoughts turned to the new government
for America. As she realized that her husband would help
decide how a new political
system would work, she
wrote her most famous letter to John:

> In the new code of laws
> which I suppose it will
> be necessary for you to
> make, I desire you
> would remember the
> ladies and be more
> generous and favorable

*Mercy Warren, though many years
older than Abigail, became one of
Abigail's greatest friends.*

to them than your ancestors. Do not put such unlimited power into the hands of the husbands. Remember, all men would be tyrants if they could. If particular care and attention is not paid to the ladies, we are determined to foment a rebellion, and will not hold ourselves bound by any laws in which we have no voice or representation."[12]

John was amused by her letter and replied, "As to your extraordinary code of laws, I cannot but laugh. We have been told that our struggle has loosed the bonds of government everywhere; . . . But your letter was the first intimation that another tribe, more numerous and powerful than all the rest, were grown discontented."[13]

Abigail's view was radical for her time, when women were not allowed to own property, or even to have opinions. She believed that American women should have a legal existence apart from their husbands, and did her best to make her own husband aware of the importance of women in society.

Independence—And Another Epidemic

In the spring of 1776, Massachusetts was in the clutches of a smallpox epidemic. Abigail took the children to Boston to be inoculated against the dreaded disease. They stayed at Uncle Isaac Smith's home.

Soon after their arrival, they received news of the Declaration of Independence. Abigail heard the Declaration of Independence read from the balcony of the statehouse in Boston. The cheering crowd rang bells and fired cannons to celebrate.

Soon Abigail did not have time to think about independence. Her whole world revolved around smallpox. She and John Quincy became only slightly ill from the inoculation

The Declaration of Independence

John Adams, who was part of the committee assigned to write the Declaration, wrote to Abigail, "Yesterday [July 2] the greatest Question was decided, which ever was debated in America . . . A Resolution was passed without one dissenting Colony 'that these united Colonies, are, and of right ought to be free and independent States."[14] John Adams thought the second day of July, when Congress voted to declare independence, would be celebrated every year with a great anniversary festival. The resolution was signed two days later, however, so Americans celebrate Independence Day on July 4.

they all received, but poor Nabby had six hundred or seven hundred eruptions of blisters on her skin. She survived but was left scarred for life. Charles was delirious for two days with a fever. In Philadelphia, John Adams was afraid to open letters from Boston. He had terrible fears that one of the children had died. When he finally heard that Charles was recovering, he wrote, "I did not know what fast Hold that little Prattler Charles had upon me before."[15]

Another Pregnancy

In November 1776, John came home again before leaving for the next session of Congress. This time, he would return to Baltimore, since Congress expected the British to occupy Philadelphia. When he left, he knew Abigail was again pregnant. They both hoped for another daughter.[16]

Abigail Adams was present when the Declaration of Independence, which her husband helped write, was read to crowds in Boston.

Although it was not a new experience for her to have a baby when John was away, Abigail became depressed as her delivery time approached. She worried more after a neighbor died in childbirth. What if she died? Who would care for the children? On July 9, she wrote, "I was last night taken with a shaking fit, and am very apprehensive that a life was lost."[17]

Her apprehensions proved to be true. On July 13, John Thaxter, the boys' tutor, wrote to John:

Sir:
The day before Yesterday Mrs. Adams was delivered of a daughter; but it grieves me to add, Sir, that it was still born [dead at birth]. It was an exceeding fine looking Child.[18]

Abigail was shocked, and the children were in a daze.

John was overcome with sadness. He wrote: "Never in my whole life was my heart affected with such emotions. Devoutly do I return thanks to God, whose kind providence has preserved to me a life [Abigail's] that is dearer to me than all other blessings in the world." He went on to say, "Is it not unaccountable, that one should feel so strong an Affection for an Infant, that one has never seen, nor shall see? Yet I must confess to you, the Loss of this sweet little Girl, has most tenderly and sensibly affected me."[19]

As Abigail recovered from the loss of her little daughter, she turned her interest toward the struggle for independence. She asked John for a map so she could follow the progress of the war.

One day, a letter came from John Lovell, John's fellow Boston delegate to the Continental Congress. Congress was now acting as the unofficial governing body for the united colonies. Abigail was seized by panic over the letter, afraid Lovell was writing to tell her that John was ill or even dead. She finally got up the courage to read it. Lovell had heard she wanted a map, so he sent one. Abigail thought that the enclosed note was a little too affectionate, since he spoke of her beauty and her charms. However, she told John merely that Lovell had sent her a "very polite Letter."[20]

During the winter of 1777–1778, British General William Howe's troops occupied Philadelphia, while General Washington's poorly clad army suffered from terrible cold at Valley Forge, Pennsylvania. On October 17, 1777, the Americans scored an important victory at Saratoga, New York. British General John Burgoyne was forced to surrender five thousand troops. Abigail took Nabby into Boston to join the celebration there.

On November 27, John Adams came home. Congress had voted leave for him and Sam Adams to visit their families.

Both John and Abigail hoped he was home for good this time. He actually considered not returning to Congress. He decided to practice law again to bolster their finances and went to New Hampshire to try a case.

Commissioner to France

Soon after John left, a packet of letters arrived from Congress. Abigail opened it to see if she needed to forward it to John in New Hampshire. She was shocked to learn that John had been elected commissioner to France. He was to help fellow politicians Benjamin Franklin and Arthur Lee negotiate an alliance with the French. The Americans thought that if France were their ally, the British would be more likely to give in to their demand for independence.

John hurried back to Braintree. Together, he and Abigail suffered over whether John should accept the position or stay at home. He finally decided he must go and serve his country. Abigail, although everything in her wanted him to stay, did not have the heart to ask him to. She knew he played an important role in the affairs of their country. She would again remain in Braintree.

6

HOME ALONE

Although John could not afford to take the whole family
to France, he decided to take John Quincy, who was
now ten.

Abigail hated to see her son go. She felt she needed him
at home. He helped with chores and rode to and from
Boston with letters. Besides, she and the other children
would miss him. She was glad, though, that he could spend
time with his father, and she knew travel would be good for
him. John Quincy reminded her that the new country
would need diplomats after the war and this would give
him training.[1]

Abigail said her good-byes at home. She thought it
would be too painful to watch them board the ship. John
gave her a tiny locket with a picture of a lonely woman
watching a ship sail off. She said she watched them ride out
of sight "with full heart and weeping eye."[2]

Young John Quincy Adams would go with his father to Europe to gain valuable diplomatic experience.

Anxious Waiting

Then the waiting began. Abigail heard that the *Boston*, the ship on which her husband and son had sailed, had been captured and taken to England. She was frantic. She did not know what to believe. She nearly gave up hope that her husband and son were alive. She even stopped writing to them. "My Heart so much misgave me that I knew not how to hold my pen, and the distracting thought of not knowing where to find you withheld my hand," she later wrote to John.[3]

Finally, a London newspaper reported the safe arrival in France of John Adams and his son. On June 30—nearly five months after they had sailed—Abigail received her first letter from her husband.

He told her the *Boston* had captured the British ship *Martha*. John had insisted on remaining on deck during the fighting, although Captain Samuel Tucker had ordered him to stay below. According to John's memoirs, the captain bellowed, "Why are you here, sir? I have bidden you go below a dozen times in the hour. Why are you here? I am commanded by the Continental Congress to carry you in safety to Europe, and by thunder I will do it!"[4] With that, he seized John and dragged him below.

John wrote, "My Johnny's behavior gave me a satisfaction that I cannot express; fully sensible of our danger, he was constantly endeavoring to bear it with a manly patience, very attentive to me, and his thoughts constantly running in a serious strain."[5]

Father and son arrived in Paris, France, on March 30, 1778, six weeks after leaving Boston Harbor. On June 3, John still had not heard from Abigail. He wrote to her, "It is now the 3d of June, and I have not received a Line, nor heard a Word, directly nor indirectly, concerning you since my departure . . . I assure you I feel a great deal of Anxiety."[6]

The whole time John Adams was in France, only a fraction of the letters he and Abigail wrote arrived at their destinations. Some were lost. Others were thrown overboard when American ships were captured by the British.

Upon his arrival, there was little for John Adams to do. A treaty had already been signed between France and America before he got to Paris. As a result of the new alliance with France, a fleet of French ships was sent to Boston. Comte d'Estaing, chief officer of the French fleet in Boston, invited Abigail to dine with him on board, and she entertained him and his officers several times.

Lonely Times at Home

Despite her interesting visitors, Abigail was lonely. She had rented the farm to two young men who took full responsibility for doing the work and paying the taxes. Although she still had one household to manage, she had more time to miss her husband and son.

Nabby, who was twelve, was attending school in Boston, so only Charles and Thomas remained at home. Nabby came home for Christmas, then spent several weeks with Mercy Warren. Abigail missed her daughter but thought the visit would be good for her.

Charles was eight, and it was time for him to begin grammar school. There was no good school in Braintree, so Abigail sent him to stay with her sister Elizabeth and her husband, John Shaw, in Haverhill. Shaw, a minister and schoolteacher, would tutor him.

She was delighted when her brother William's two-year-old daughter came to live with her. William had been a disappointment to the family. He was an alcoholic, he had failed in business, and he had barely eked out a living on his farm for himself, his wife, and their children. Abigail had always wanted another daughter, so she enjoyed caring for little Louisa.

Continued Correspondence

To keep up on political affairs, Abigail corresponded with friends in Congress. John Thaxter, now a clerk for Congress, had lived with the family while he served as John's law clerk and had tutored the Adams boys while John was in Philadelphia. He wrote about the war, sent Abigail books to read, and asked her opinion on political matters. Abigail also corresponded with James Lovell, who, after a time, became quite familiar in his letters. His flattering phrases and compliments were not quite proper. She scolded him but continued to write to him anyway.[7]

As their time apart went on, Abigail became quite depressed about her husband's letters. His few letters had been short and unemotional, unlike the affectionate letters he had sent her from Philadelphia. She finally wrote him a scathing letter accusing him of neglecting her. She wrote, "By Heaven if you could you have changed Hearts with some frozen Laplander [person from northern Scandinavia or Russia] or made a voyage to a region that has chilld every Drop of your Blood," she wrote.[8]

A few days later, she received three letters from John at once and learned he had received only one of the many letters she had written. John did not appreciate "this complaining style." He said he had written several answers but had not sent any of them. He wrote,

> One was angry, another was full of Greif, and the third with Melancholy, so that I burnt them all. —If you write me in this style I shall leave of writing intirely, it kills me. Can Professions of Esteem be Wanting from me to you? Can Protestation of affection be necessary? . . . Am I not wretched Enough, in this Banishment, without this . . . I beg you would never more write to me in such a strain for it really makes me unhappy.[9]

John Quincy copied the letter for his father, then added his own little note to Abigail: "My Pappa cannot write but very little because he has so many other things to think of . . . and when you receive them you complain . . . and it really hurts him."[10] After getting his scolding letter, she tried not to complain about John's correspondence.

Progress in Paris

John was having a difficult time in Paris. Benjamin Franklin and Arthur Lee, the other American commissioners, were bitter enemies. John believed their quarrels hampered the effectiveness of American negotiations. He thought a single commissioner would be more effective. He wrote to Sam Adams, urging Congress to reduce the Paris personnel to one.

In February 1779, word came that Franklin had been appointed the sole minister to France. John Adams and

Benjamin Franklin, one of the commissioners originally sent to work with John Adams, was eventually named sole commissioner in France.

Arthur Lee were relieved of their duties. Lee was named minister to Spain, but John was given no orders. He was at loose ends, so decided to go home, but it was June 18 before he and John Quincy could set sail for Boston.

The last letters Abigail received from John in Europe were dated February, and it was now summer. She knew Franklin had been appointed sole minister but did not know where John was. While she was trying to figure out where he might be, he and Johnny appeared on the beach at Braintree, having been rowed ashore from the ship *Sensible*. The family was reunited at last. Unfortunately, their togetherness would not last long.

7

ALONE AGAIN

When John got home, he and Abigail could not spend enough time together. They took long walks, visited friends and relatives, and worked on the farm. Both hoped he was home to stay. Abigail was now thirty-five, and John was forty-four.

John was elected to the Massachusetts constitutional convention. He was on the committee to draft and write a new state constitution. When he came home on the weekends, he discussed important points with Abigail. She read each page as he wrote it and was happy to talk politics with him again.

Back to Europe
In October, Abigail's whole world fell apart. Congress named John minister plenipotentiary to negotiate treaties of peace and commerce with Great Britain. He had to go

back to France as soon as possible. But this time, he would not have to share his commission with Benjamin Franklin or anyone else.

Abigail was crushed but agreed that the country needed John and that he must accept the mission. This time, he took both John Quincy and Charles with him.

John Thaxter would serve as John's private secretary, and Francis Dana, a young lawyer from Boston, was secretary to the delegation.

John wrote Abigail a comforting note just before they sailed: "We shall yet be happy, I hope and pray, and I don't doubt it . . . Yours, ever, ever yours."[1]

The group boarded the ship *Sensible* in Boston. It was a relatively fast and easy voyage. John Quincy and Charles did lessons on board the ship, learning Latin and French.

The ship sprang a leak off the coast of Spain, so the captain put in at a nearby port. Rather than wait two months for the ship to be repaired, John decided to travel overland to France. They set out through the mountains in the dead of winter with carriages, mules, and a guide. The roads were so steep and narrow that they often had to get out and walk. They finally arrived in Paris on February 9, 1780.

Abigail's Business

Meanwhile, Abigail waited and worried. At the end of February, she learned that her husband and sons had landed safely in Spain.

She tried to be cheerful and was careful this time not to criticize John's letters. The two had discussed her feelings and the angry letters while John was home. He had assured her of his love, and she had resigned herself to being alone.

Abigail missed John and John Quincy, but she could hardly bear to be parted from nine-year-old Charles. Everybody loved the little blond boy with the chubby face and sweet voice. She missed John Thaxter, too. He had been almost like a son to her, and she had depended on him the first time John went to France.

Abigail had always been good at business, and she supplemented the family income by selling European goods John sent her. He bought cloth, handkerchiefs, ribbons, laces, and tea at low prices, and she sold them for a profit to friends and neighbors. Before long, she knew exactly which things sold best and sent him specific orders.

Soon, John suggested that Abigail order directly from the merchants in Holland, Spain, and France. Occasionally, Mercy Warren or Uncle Isaac sold some of the items for her.

Sometimes, Abigail asked for things for herself and Nabby—silk gloves, pretty cloth, and a little lace. She told John, "a little of what you call frippery is very necessary towards looking like the rest of the world." She told him that Nabby asked her to assure Pappa that she "has no passion for dress further than what he would approve." She just wanted to look "like those of her own age."[2]

John's Problems in Europe

The situation was not going well in Paris. John did not like or trust the French foreign minister, Comte de Vergennes. The comte wrote a letter to Benjamin Franklin complaining about John. Franklin sent it on to Congress.

Although John had no authority to negotiate there, he went to Holland, thinking an alliance with that country would benefit the United States. He told Abigail that the people there were thrifty, industrious, moral, and learned. He convinced the Dutch that America was able and determined to persevere in the fight for independence, and they were impressed with him.

John Thaxter took the Adams boys to the University of Leyden, near Amsterdam, where they were both admitted. Charles was underage, but the Adams boys were already so proficient in Latin and Greek that the university took him anyway.

John got word on September 17 that Congress had appointed him the official representative to Holland. He immediately tried to negotiate an alliance and a loan. When he had not succeeded by the end of the year, he became despondent. He did not write to Abigail for three months.

Abigail was lonely, but she comforted herself by reading and rereading his past letters. She did not get mail from her husband or sons for almost a year. Most of her information about them during that time came from newspapers and from her correspondents in Congress, John Lovell and Elbridge Gerry.

She did not like what she read. Congress had appointed four additional ministers to help with the peace treaty and had revoked John's commission to negotiate a treaty of commerce. It seemed that Comte de Vergennes and Franklin were trying to ruin his reputation. People thought John had a self-important attitude, and many did not like him.

John had been gone almost two years, and the war was nearing a climax. On October 19, 1781, George Washington's troops trapped British General Charles Cornwallis's forces on the Yorktown peninsula. Cornwallis surrendered eight thousand troops. This would prove to be the last major battle of the war, although the official end would not come until the peace treaty was signed in 1783.

When Abigail finally heard from John, she learned that Johnny was on his way to Russia. He was sent along with Francis Dana, who was to serve as minister to the court of Catherine the Great, ruler of Russia. John Quincy would serve as Dana's secretary and translator. It was quite an adventure for a fourteen-year-old boy.

Charles Comes Home

In September, John informed Abigail that Charles had been ill, was homesick, and missed his mother. John had decided to send the boy home. Abigail heard nothing more about Charles's whereabouts until December, when she heard he had been detained in Bilboa, Spain. She wrote to John, "Alass my dear I am much afflicted with a disorder call'd the *Heartache*, nor can any remedy be found in America, it must be collected from Holland, Peterburg and Bilboa."[3]

Finally, Charles arrived home in January 1782. Abigail was worried when he told her his father had been seriously ill with a "nervous fever."[4] John had been in a coma for five days, but John Thaxter had nursed him back to health. It was two months before he was well enough to work.

In April, John finally achieved Dutch recognition for the new United States. Abigail and Nabby clamored to join him in Europe. He wanted them to come but thought he would return home himself as soon as a peace treaty was signed with Great Britain.

Worries About Nabby

Abigail wanted to go to Europe because Nabby was getting serious about a romance with a young man named Royall Tyler. Tyler had a reputation for having wasted a lot of

This portrait of Nabby Adams was painted by artist Mather Brown in 1785.

money and time. He seemed to have reformed and was now a serious young lawyer. Abigail, however, thought Nabby, at eighteen, was too young for marriage. By this time, Nabby was tall, blond, and beautiful, with cool gray eyes and a quiet demeanor.[5] Abigail thought her too passive and unemotional, but John told her to stop criticizing their daughter. He said her quiet manner was her most attractive quality, and even hinted that Abigail would do well to follow her example![6]

John, too, was concerned about the relationship between Tyler and his only daughter. He wrote, "My child is too young for such thoughts." He told his daughter, "Regard the Honour and moral Character of the Man more than all other Circumstances."[7]

Meanwhile, John Quincy was on his way back from St. Petersburg. The boy finally arrived at The Hague, the Dutch seat of government, on April 21, 1783. His father was still in Paris, waiting for the peace treaty to be signed.

While John remained in France, Abigail was having her own problem at home. In September 1783, her father died. As had happened so often throughout her marriage, she was left to grieve alone once again.

Also in September, Great Britain signed the peace treaty acknowledging the United States as an independent country. John expected to come home after learning of the development, but Congress instead appointed him to negotiate a treaty of commerce (trade) with England.

An Invitation to Europe

Immediately, John wrote to Abigail, saying, "Will you come to me this fall . . . with my dear Nabby?"[8] His letter did not arrive until the end of the year. Abigail refused to cross the ocean during the winter, when the sea is roughest, but she said they would come in the spring.

Her sister Mary agreed to take care of John's mother, since Abigail would not be there to do it. Sister Elizabeth would take Thomas and Charles to live with her, and Elizabeth's husband, John Shaw, would help prepare them for Harvard. Abigail's biggest concern was seven-year-old Louisa Smith, the niece who had lived with her for the past five years. The little girl remembered no other home and was devastated at the thought of her aunt's leaving. Abigail promised that Louisa would be able to live with the Adamses again when they returned.

Now Abigail and Nabby waited eagerly for spring.

8

ABIGAIL GOES
TO EUROPE

In spring 1785, Abigail booked passage on the ship *Active*.
Charles and Thomas had already settled in with
Elizabeth and John Shaw. Abigail knew Elizabeth would
love and watch over them.

Mary would care for John's mother. Susanna Adams
was very upset that Abigail was leaving, so she did not tell
her the exact day they were leaving. When the elderly lady
saw Abigail at her door, dressed in traveling clothes, she
broke into tears. "O! Why did you not tell me you was
going so soon? Final day! I take my last leave; I shall never
see you again. Carry my last blessing to my Son."[1] With
great difficulty, Abigail left the weeping woman.

Nabby and Royall Tyler exchanged keepsakes, said tear-
ful farewells, and vowed to love one another forever.

Abigail and Nabby boarded the *Active* on Sunday, June
18, 1784. They had a good bit of luggage, including a cow

to provide them with milk, cream, and butter during the voyage. The ship was small but was supposed to be extra safe because of its copper bottom. The eleven passengers ate in one large cabin and spent most of their time there. Two eight-foot-square cabins served as women's staterooms.

Abigail and Nabby were violently seasick for two days. Abigail was glad John could not see her in such a state. She wrote to Mary, "Of this I am very sure, that no lady would ever wish a second time to try the sea, were the objects of her pursuit within the reach of a land journey."[2]

The food was even worse than she had expected, but worse yet to her were the dirt and the smell. After the sea calmed down, Abigail proceeded to clean up the ship. She had the crew working with brushes, mops, and scrapers. Within a few hours, there was a noticeable improvement. Her next project was the galley, or kitchen. She taught the cook to make several recipes, and even made some desserts herself. She spoke of the milk pail being "enough to poison anyone."[3]

They spotted land on July 19, exactly four weeks after leaving Boston. "You will hardly wonder at the joy we felt this day seeing the cliffs of Dover [on the south coast of England]," she wrote to Mary.[4]

A gale-force wind rose, whipping up six-foot-high waves. After waiting three days for the wind to subside, they decided to chance going ashore. Abigail and Nabby got into a small boat, each clinging to a male passenger so they would not fall overboard. The crashing waves soaked them thoroughly before they made it to land.

When they arrived, they learned that John was in Holland. John Quincy had been waiting for them for a month and had just gone back to his father.

Their hotel overlooked the Thames River. They had "a fine drawing-room, genteely furnished, and a large bed-room."[5] The cost included the services of a cook, waiter, and maid.

Abigail wrote to John, "Heaven be praised, I am with our daughter safely landed upon the British Shore."[6] The weather was sunny and cool, and while they waited to hear from John, she and Nabby enjoyed shopping and sight-seeing. Soon John's answer came: "Your Letter of the 23rd has made me the happiest Man upon Earth. I am twenty Years younger than I was yesterday."[7] He could not come yet but would send John Quincy. Abigail and Nabby went to see a portrait that the young artist John Singleton Copley had recently painted of John, and Abigail pro-claimed it an excellent likeness.

Family Reunion

On July 30, a servant rushed into their room. "Young Mr. Adams is come!" he announced.[8] Abigail would not have recognized the tall young man. His eyes looked familiar, but John Quincy had grown from a boy into a man in the four years since she had last seen him.

Styles in London
Abigail and Nabby were amazed at the lack of style and elegance in the dress in London. She commented that "A common straw hat, no cap, with only a ribbon upon the crown" was suitable for going calling.[9] Dress in the colonies was more formal, and a cap, often made of lace, was always worn.

"Oh my Mamma! And my Dear Sister!" he cried, rushing to hug them both.[10] Tears ran down Abigail's face as she embraced her son. She wrote to Mary, "I think you do not approve the word feelings, but I know not what to Substitute in lieu, or even to describe mine."[11]

Eight days later, when her father arrived, Nabby wrote in her journal,

> At 12, returned to our apartments. . . . I saw upon the table a hat with two books in it; every thing appeared altered. . . . "What is this appearance of strangeness?— Whose hat is that in the other room?—Whose trunk is this?—Whose sword and cane?—It is my father's," said I. "Where is he?"
> "In the room above."
> Up I flew, and to his chamber. . . . [He] received me with all the tenderness of an affectionate parent after so long an absence.[12]

Abigail wrote to Mary about her reunion with John: "Poets and painters wisely draw a veil over those Scenes which surpass the pen of one and the pencil of the other; we were indeed a very very happy family once more met together after a Separation of four years."[13]

On to Paris

They left the next day for Paris, where John met daily with Benjamin Franklin and Thomas Jefferson, another American statesman. Abigail was not impressed with Paris. She said, "I have smelt it. . . . It is the very dirtiest place I ever saw."[14]

Luckily, she did not have to live there. John rented a huge house just outside Auteuil. It was close to the Bois de Bologne, a huge park with woods and paths where he walked every day. Abigail loved the garden but thought the house was too big and badly arranged. The rooms were drafty, and there were no carpets. She hated the red tile floors, which were hard to clean. The servants were lazy, and Abigail had a real struggle keeping the thirty-room house clean. However, she loved her bedroom, which had an adjoining "apartment" overlooking the gardens.[15] She enjoyed reading and writing letters in the little private area.

The French women were extremely fashionable. People were friendly, but Abigail did not approve of the fact that many French people seemed to live their lives only for pleasure. A deeply religious woman, she was shocked that Sunday was not taken seriously as a day of worship there, as it was back home in the United States.

A French maid, Pauline, powdered and dressed Abigail's and Nabby's hair every day, and they practiced their French with her. They became very close, and when Abigail and Nabby left Paris, Abigail presented Pauline with a little songbird she loved.

There was plenty to do in Paris. Abigail loved the opera, and once she got used to the skimpy clothing worn by the performers, she began to enjoy the ballet. The Adamses also attended plays.

A Balloon Launching

While living at Auteuil in France, the Adamses went to watch a balloon launching at Tuilleries, near Paris. The first successful hot-air balloon had been invented in 1782 by the Montgolfier brothers, so flying in a balloon was still a new and exciting phenomenon.

Making New Friends

Abigail and John called on Marie Adrienne, the wife of the Marquis de Lafayette, a young Frenchman who had fought in the American Revolution. Abigail liked Marie Adrienne, who was a strong supporter of American independence, and, like Abigail, preferred plain fashions.

Abigail also became close friends with Thomas Jefferson. They shared a love for books and quiet family life. She described him as "one of the choice ones of the earth."[16]

In May 1785, John was appointed the first American ambassador to the Court of St. James in London. Abigail was happy to go back to England. Her only regret was leaving Thomas Jefferson behind. Jefferson held a dinner to celebrate John's appointment, and his own as minister to France.

John Quincy set sail for Boston. He would finish his education at Harvard. After being with his father for so long, the parting was difficult. But it was even harder for John Quincy to part with his sister, Nabby. They had become close friends in the year they had been back together. She gave him a packet of

Abigail Adams became close friends with Thomas Jefferson, despite the fact that he and her husband were sometimes political rivals.

letters to deliver to Royall Tyler and asked him to find out why Tyler had not written.

A Meeting With the King

Soon after their arrival in England, the family was presented to King George III. John had a private audience on June 1, a rare honor for someone who had so recently been part of a revolutionary movement against the king. Abigail had helped him memorize a speech. He bought new clothes and learned the etiquette of approaching and addressing a king.

As a farmer and country lawyer, John felt hesitant about meeting a king. However, the king was surprisingly respectful and friendly, saying, "I was the first, sir, and the last, to resist the notion of American independence. I will be the first to welcome independent America's representative. I am glad, sir, that your country's choice has fallen upon you."[17]

Abigail and Nabby's preparations for their meeting with the king were more elaborate than John's. A dressmaker made them new dresses. Abigail asked that her gown be "elegant, but plain as I could possibly appear, with decency." The result was a silk dress trimmed with white crepe, lilac ribbons, and lace.[18] Nabby's dress was similar. They spent all morning dressing and having their hair done. Abigail wore a lace cap with two white plumes over her curls.

They felt ridiculous as they stepped into the carriage with difficulty. Their hoops barely fit through the door, and the feathers on their hats brushed the ceiling.

More than two hundred people waited in the great reception room to meet the royal family. They stood for four hours, waiting. Abigail wrote and told John Quincy she

The Adamses were given the rare honor of being introduced to King George III of England.

must be a fool to stand four hours, waiting for royalty to speak to her. Nabby wrote that the whole ceremony was ridiculous, and the Prince of Wales looked "stuffed."[19]

Life in London

They rented a large townhouse in Grosvenor Square, in a fashionable part of London. The house faced that of former Prime Minister Lord North. Jokingly, Abigail wrote to a friend that, "We have not taken a side with Lord North, but are still opposite to him."[20]

Americans in London enjoyed gathering at the Adams house. The group included artists John Singleton Copley, John Trumbull, Benjamin West, and Mather Brown. John sat for a portrait by Brown. He was so pleased that he had Brown paint Abigail and Nabby as well.

Life in London was very different from life in Paris. Abigail had a broader social life now. As the official United States representative to England, John was expected to entertain a lot. Abigail acted as hostess and was also expected to attend receptions, call on people, and receive visitors.

The theaters offered a large variety of entertainment, from Shakespeare to Italian opera. Abigail had always loved Shakespeare, but this was the first time she had seen his plays performed. Usually, she had simply enjoyed reading the plays. She and Nabby also attended a performance of Handel's famous oratorio *The Messiah* at Westminster Abbey. "It was sublime beyond description," she wrote to Thomas Jefferson.[21]

Unlike the French, the British went to church on Sundays. The Adamses always drove to a church about six miles from London to hear Dr. Richard Price preach. His ancestors had been Puritans and he had supported the independence of the colonies.

The cost of living was higher in London than it had been in the United States or in Paris, and John and Abigail found themselves under financial stress. Congress would not finance some of the traditional events they were expected to organize, such as a dinner for other foreign ministers. The London press ridiculed the Adamses for being stingy.

The Adamses finally decided to give the dinner, no matter what they had to go without to pay for it themselves. Then, a Boston ship arrived from the West Indies. The captain gave them a giant codfish and a 114-pound turtle, which was served to their guests.

News From Home

Everyone was excited when a packet of letters from John Quincy arrived. His mother wrote, "Up we all jumped. Your sister seized hold of a letter and cried, 'My brother, my brother!' . . . The chocolate grew cold, the teapot was forgotten, the bread and butter went down uneaten, yet nobody felt the loss of breakfast."[22]

Nabby was upset that summer of 1785. She was thinking seriously of breaking her engagement to Royall Tyler. She heard that he had told everyone she was chasing him and that he had shared her letters with friends. He had even opened and read a letter that she had asked him to deliver to Betsey Cranch.

Finally, in August, she told him it was over and sent back his letters and the small portrait he had given her when she left for Europe. She asked her friends and family never to mention him again.

Nabby was soon attracted to her father's secretary, Colonel William Smith. He often visited their home and had fallen in love with Nabby, although he knew she was engaged. John and Abigail were afraid that, if Nabby began dating Smith, it would look as though he had caused the broken engagement. To avoid this, John sent Smith to Prussia to observe military demonstrations.

Nabby helped her father with his correspondence while William was gone. When he returned, she was surprised how happy she was to see him. By February, she and William were engaged. Abigail was pleased. She wrote to John Quincy that Colonel Smith was "like to become your brother."

Political Problems in America

Meanwhile, things were not going well at home. The British would not let the United States trade with the West Indies, a group of islands between North and South America. The West Indies had always been one of the Americans' main sources of imports. Also, the British had to pay high taxes on American goods. John was trying to negotiate a commercial treaty that would solve these problems.

Disturbing news soon came from Massachusetts. A group of poor farmers had lost their farms due to the tough financial times that followed the end of the revolution. These farmers soon turned to violence to try to get the government to help them with their troubles. In an uprising known as Shays' Rebellion, the farmers, armed with guns, had tried to keep the courts from meeting and sheriffs from selling the property confiscated from farmers who could not afford to pay their debts. Though the rebellion was quickly put down, it showed a need for a stronger government for the United States—one that could prevent

Abigail Adams was outraged at the violent tactics used by the farmers in Massachusetts in Shays' Rebellion. Some members of the farmers' movement are seen here, attacking a tax collector.

such terrible financial problems and future revolts from occurring.

Abigail was horrified by the news of Shays' Rebellion. She wrote to Jefferson, describing the men as "ignorant, wrestless, desperadoes, without conscience or principals."[24] She was not happy with his reply. It said, "The spirit of resistance to government is so valuable on certain occasions, that I wish it always kept alive. It will often be exercised when wrong, but better so than not to be exercised at all. I like a little rebellion now and then."[25]

Partly as a result of Shays' Rebellion, Congress decided to call a Constitutional Convention to work on changing and improving the American system of government. The convention would meet in May 1787. John could not be there, but he would still leave his mark on the new constitution. The delegates used the Massachusetts Constitution he had helped write eight years before as one of their models.

Family Ties

By now, all three Adams boys were at Harvard. Abigail cautioned John Quincy about being overly critical of his fellow students and teachers. "Reflect that you have had the greater opportunities of seeing the world," she wrote.[26]

Abigail's sisters wrote to her to tell her about the progress of her others sons, too. They wrote that Tommy was solid and practical, while Charles was very social. Mary wrote that Charles was really too handsome![27]

As always, Abigail's sisters were her source of comfort and help. Now that the boys were in college and Abigail away in Europe, Mary took over the role of mothering them. She lived close to Cambridge, where Harvard is located, and her son Billy was also a student at the college. The Adams boys spent their vacations with her.

Abigail and John paid her sisters for the boys' room and board, but Abigail knew that nothing could repay them for all the love and care they showed her nephews. She tried to make it up to Mary and Elizabeth by sending them and their daughters little luxuries they could not get in Boston, such as silk for dresses, ribbons, bonnets, and sandals.

On June 12, 1786, Nabby and William Smith were married. They rented a house about a mile and a half from her parents. John missed her so much that, the day after she left, he knocked on Abigail's door at 11:00 A.M. and announced, "Well, I have been to see them."[28]

In April 1787, Nabby gave birth to a little boy, named William after his father. Abigail was only forty-two, but she loved being a grandmother. She wrote to her niece, Lucy Cranch "I feel already as fond of him as if he was my own son."[29]

In the spring of 1787, Thomas Jefferson's eight-year-old daughter, Polly, arrived in England. Polly had been unhappy about leaving home, but her father wanted her with him and her older sister in France. He asked Abigail to look after her until he could send someone to bring her to France. Abigail was delighted.

Polly had become attached to the ship's captain during the voyage to Europe, and she cried when she had to leave him. However, Abigail soon made her forget her tears. They became very fond of each other, and Abigail took the little girl shopping and to an amusement park.

"Books are her delight," she wrote to Jefferson, "and I have furnished her out a little library, and she reads to me by the hour with great distinctness, and comments on what she reads with much propriety."[30]

When Polly left for France, she wept, saying to Abigail, "Oh! Now I have learned to love you, why will they take me from you?"[31]

Johnny, now grown up and calling himself John Quincy Adams, graduated from Harvard in July. Abigail wished with all her heart that she could be there. She wrote, "Neither time or Distance have . . . diminished the . . . affection which I bear you—you are ever upon my heart and mind."[32] Billy Cranch, Abigail's nephew, also graduated, and Mary made a huge plum cake for the commencement party.

Time to Go Home

Sad news came in July. Abigail's brother, William, had died at the age of forty-one. He had lived an unhappy, troubled life. Abigail felt sorry for him and his family.

John and Abigail wanted to go home. His commission would expire the next spring, so he wrote Congress and asked them not to renew it.

Cotton Tufts, Abigail's uncle, wrote that a large house they both liked was for sale in Braintree. John told him to buy it, since they needed a bigger home, if only to accommodate the many books he had bought in Europe.

Abigail's Brother's Life
William Smith, known as Billy, led a disappointing life. He refused to attend Harvard, failed in business, and had a wife and several children, whom he had difficulty supporting. He battled alcoholism for years and finally died in 1787, alone and far from home.

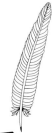

In April, they set sail for America. Abigail's only regret was parting with Nabby and little William, who would live near William's family in New York. Abigail had always wanted to travel, especially to England. But now her travels were over, and she was glad to be going home.

9

THE VICE PRESIDENT'S WIFE

J ohn and Abigail Adams returned to a hero's welcome in Boston. A cheering crowd of thousands met them at the wharf. John Hancock, governor of Massachusetts, took them to his home on Beacon Hill. He entertained them lavishly, and they were reunited with their three sons.

They felt flattered but a little uneasy. Hancock wanted to escort them by carriage to Braintree. The citizens of Braintree planned to march partway to Boston to meet them. The Adamses were not comfortable with this grand display, so they did not tell anyone when they were leaving.

A New Home

Their new home was not ready, so they stayed for a while with John's brother, Peter, while workers finished their home. Abigail wrote to Nabby that the "Garden was a wilderness & the House a mere Barrack."[1] Carpenters and

John Hancock, famous patriot and close friend of the Adams family, tried to give John and Abigail a spectacular welcome home celebration.

masons swarmed over the house until she almost wished they had not bought it. Their furniture, which they had shipped from London, arrived damaged. Despite these problems, John named the farm Peacefield, to reflect his mood when he was there.

Abigail had remembered the house as being large and elegant. But compared to the mansions they had occupied in France and England, this seven-room house seemed small indeed. "In height and breadth, it feels like a wren's house," she wrote.[2]

Abigail hoped living abroad had not changed her. She had written to Mary, "Believe me I am not in the least alterd except that I wear my Hair drest and powdered, and am two years older, & somewhat fatter."[3]

Her tastes, however, had changed somewhat, after living in luxury for two years. Over the next few years, Abigail converted the new house into an impressive home, doubling the size of it.

Election

John was being considered for the vice presidency. Everyone knew George Washington would be elected president, since he had led the nation to independence and was still extremely popular. John considered himself too honest to be popular.

Abigail went to New York to see Nabby's new baby, John. While there, she learned more about her husband's chances for the vice presidency. "I suppose you will tell me I have no Buisness with politics," she wrote to John Adams. "I design to be vastly prudent I assure you [and] hear all & say little!"[4] It was not like Abigail to say little, but she did not want John to appear eager for the office. At the time, it was considered rather vulgar to actually pursue a political office.

According to the procedure set forth in the new Constitution, each elector cast two ballots, without designating which was for the presidency and which for the vice presidency. The man with the most votes would become president; the other would be vice president.

As expected, Washington was elected president. John was elected vice president. It was a great honor and a chance for him to serve his country yet again. He left right away, as the new government needed to get started as soon as possible.

John rented a house at Richmond Hill, just outside the city of New York, where the United States capital was then located. Abigail wrote to her sister Mary: "The house in which we reside is situated upon a hill . . . In front of the house, the noble Hudson rolls his majestic waves." She loved the house, the gardens, and the view of the river. She wrote about the "lovely variety" of birds that sang to her every morning.[5]

They shipped furniture from Braintree to furnish the house. This was a problem, because they would need the furniture at Braintree when they went home during congressional recesses. But on John's small salary, they could not afford to furnish another house.

Abigail, Charles, and Louisa Smith had traveled by stagecoach to Providence, Rhode Island, then by boat to New York. During five days of storms, Abigail was seasick and frightened, and she vowed never to "embark upon the water" again.[6]

Vice President's Hostess

As wife of the vice president, Abigail was obligated to make and receive many social calls. She learned that it was acceptable to make a visit when someone was out, simply leaving a calling card. So she made all her visits in the evenings, when the ladies were seldom at home. Otherwise, she knew all her time would be taken up making calls. As the vice president's wife, she was also expected to be at home to callers for some part of every day. She agreed to this custom, but she reserved Sundays for the family alone.

Soon after Abigail's arrival, she and John called on the Washingtons. The two couples became good friends and visited each other frequently. Abigail and Martha Washington were joint hostesses at a weekly "levee," or open house. Each visitor was announced, the ladies curtseyed to Martha Washington, and the President spoke to each visitor.

Abigail also invited members of Congress to dinner at the Adams house. The dining room seated twenty-four, so it took a month to entertain them all. Luckily, most of the men had left their families at home.

At the end of September 1789, Congress adjourned, having set up the executive departments, planned the federal judicial system, and approved the Bill of Rights. This

Martha Washington (right), as wife of the President, hosted many public functions. Abigail Adams sometimes hosted these functions with Martha.

was made up of the first ten amendments to the Constitution, which many people thought were necessary to ensure citizens' rights. Abigail did not want to move the furniture for such a short time, so she remained at Richmond Hill. John visited his mother for a few weeks, then returned in December.

Personal Worries

That spring, Abigail came down with a high fever. Charles also got sick, and so did the servants. Even President George Washington succumbed to the illness. For a few days, his life was in danger. Abigail worried that John would have to take over the office of president if Washington died. Luckily, Washington recovered.

Abigail was concerned about Nabby. Her husband, William, was not a good provider. Once they moved back to America, he never held a job for long. And now, Nabby was pregnant again.

In March, Abigail's younger sister, Elizabeth, had a baby girl named Abigail Adams Shaw. Elizabeth wrote Abigail that she would be supremely happy, "If some good angel would permit me to look into futurity, and I could behold my daughter like my sister, virtuous and good."[7]

In July, Abigail learned that the federal government would be moving to Philadelphia for ten years, then to a permanent site on the Potomac River, where Washington, D.C., is now located. She hated to leave Richmond Hill. She loved the house, and liked being close to Nabby and her children.

Nabby had given birth to her third child, another boy. Little Thomas seemed sickly, and Abigail worried about both Nabby and the children. Eighteen-year-old Thomas Adams graduated from Harvard and decided to live with his parents and study law. Abigail was happy to have him home.

In September 1790, John rented a house in Philadelphia, then went back to help the family move. Abigail became very ill with fever and was delirious for five days. Nabby nursed her back to health, but it was another month before she was able to make the move to Philadelphia. John and Abigail took Nabby's second son, John, with them, to make things a little easier for Nabby.

Bush Hill, their new house, needed repairs. Louisa became ill almost immediately, then Thomas. He was temporarily paralyzed and ran a high fever for eighteen days. His mother stayed by his bedside, and Dr. Benjamin Rush, an old family friend, cared for him. Meanwhile, people "were visiting us every day from 12 to 3 oclock in the midst of Rooms heepd up with Boxes, trunks, cases, &c."[8]

Life in Philadelphia

Philadelphians were friendly, and Abigail soon became a favorite. Since they lived outside of town, she did not receive as many callers as she would have otherwise.

Abigail learned that Nabby was alone with three little boys. Her husband, William, had gone to England, supposedly to try to collect some family debts. Nabby wrote that she felt alone in the world. Abigail reminded her of her own loneliness when John was away, and told her she was lucky she still had her parents for support. She told Nabby, "As to John [Nabby's son], we grow every day fonder of him. He has spent an hour this afternoon in driving his grandpapa round the room with a willow stick."[9]

All the states ratified the Constitution before Congress adjourned in May 1791. John and Abigail stopped to see Nabby on their way to Braintree. Abigail became ill with malarial fever, which she suffered nearly every year. She had first contracted the illness during the summer they lived in New York. It was carried by mosquitoes, and although there was no cure, it was rarely fatal. She spent most of the summer recuperating.

When they returned to Philadelphia, Abigail and John moved into the city so John would not have to commute. She held a levee every Monday night, and a formal dinner every Wednesday. "I feel that day a happy one that I can say I have no engagement but to my family," she wrote to Mary.[10]

John found his job as vice president frustrating and boring. All he did was preside over the Senate. He could not even vote, unless there was a tie. He told Abigail that the vice presidency was the most "insignificant office . . . ever . . . contrived."[11]

Abigail enjoyed spending time with Martha Washington. One evening when the Adamses went to a dinner party at the Washingtons' home, the President took some sugarplums off the top of a cake on the table. He gave them to Abigail to take home to her little grandson, John.[12] Washington was fond of children, even though he had none of his own.

Abigail soon became ill again. Her fever raged and she was in great pain. Her eyes were affected, so she could not read, write, or sew. Six weeks passed before she was well enough to resume her daily life.

Problems in France

Things were not going smoothly in the government, either. The French Revolution had begun in 1789. For two years, John had been writing anonymous newspaper articles about it. He thought the revolution would bring only terror, mass violence, and, eventually, the loss of the very freedom the French were seeking.

John's old friend Thomas Jefferson did not agree. He thought the French were following in the footsteps of the Americans. This disagreement led to a serious rift between the two men that would last for many years.

Abigail's biggest concern was that some of the leaders of the French Revolution were working to abolish

The French Revolution
The French Revolution started in 1789, with an uprising of the common people who were clamoring for equality. Many people wanted to abolish royalty and all noble titles to create a democratic system like that of the United States. In 1792, France declared itself a republic. Soon, however, the situation went completely out of control. People were executed for opposing the revolution. The Reign of Terror followed, during which King Louis XVI and many others were beheaded for being "enemies" of the revolution.

On July 14, 1789, the French Revolution began when peasants stormed the Bastille.

Christianity. She thought that most social and political problems were caused by neglecting religion.

Political Parties in America

In America, the two-party system was emerging, and neither John nor Abigail approved. John was a Federalist. Like other members of his party, he wanted to strengthen the federal government, with federal laws superseding those of the states. Jefferson was the leader of the Democratic-Republican party. Democratic-Republicans believed in a weak central government and more power to the states, and backed the French Revolution. Federalists thought the upper classes should rule. The Republicans were for the common man. In the spring of 1792, each party sponsored

a candidate for vice president. Both parties wanted
Washington to continue in his role as president, but the
Republicans wanted to replace John Adams with Thomas
Jefferson as vice president. Although John said he wanted
to retire, he felt it would be humiliating to lose the vice
presidency when Washington was reelected.

Abigail was sick much of that summer. Nabby's baby,
Thomas, had died, and she had gone to England with her
husband, William. After spending the summer in Braintree,
Abigail did not feel well enough to travel back to
Philadelphia with John. Besides, if he lost the election, she
would be home alone only for a short time. She wrote to
him the night before the election: "tomorrow will deter-
mine whether their Government shall stand four years
longer—or Not."

John won the election, but Abigail never returned to
Philadelphia while he was vice president. Abigail had
always had health problems. Now she seemed to pick up
every illness that came along. She was exposed to fewer
diseases on the farm in Braintree, now named Quincy after
her grandfather. The constant round of social obligations in
Philadelphia had worn down her resistance, too. In addition, it was a real financial burden on the Adamses to keep
two homes. The vice president did not receive a housing
allowance but had to pay the rent from his meager salary.
Entertaining was expensive, too. By going to the capital
alone, he could rent a room, and he did not have to entertain. Abigail and John spent summers together on the farm,
and he came home for Christmas.

Political Wife and Mother

Abigail was still interested in politics. She and John
discussed everything in letters. They were both more

convinced than ever of the importance of a strong federal government. They had similar ideas, but her beliefs were more extreme. They often came up with the same ideas at the same time, and their letters would cross. Abigail called this "the Tellegraph of the mind."[13] John said her letters "give me more entertainment than all the speeches I hear."[14]

John's mother now lived with his brother Peter up the road from Peacefield, and she visited Abigail almost daily. They were good friends, and Susanna was proud of John's accomplishments.

In 1794, John Quincy began writing letters to newspapers, defending the United States government's policy on France. Washington and Adams agreed that neutrality was necessary in the problems between France and England. John Quincy Adams became well known across the country, and George Washington noticed him. In May, the President recommended him as minister to the Netherlands.

At twenty-six, John Quincy prepared for his position abroad. His brother Thomas would serve as his secretary. Thomas hated to give up his law practice but wanted the opportunity to

John Quincy Adams was becoming a well-known political figure.

see Europe. He was the only one of the Adams children who had not been there.

Abigail and John had a happy summer at Peacefield in 1794. Soon after John returned to Philadelphia, Abigail's sister Elizabeth's husband, John Shaw, died suddenly. Abigail went to help "my dear Eliza" and her three children. She brought Elizabeth's teenage daughter, Betsey, home with her. Elizabeth thought Betsey was hard to handle and said she needed "a new mother" for a while.[15] Soon, Elizabeth married again. Her new husband, Stephen Peabody, was a minister from New Hampshire. The marriage was partly due to her desperate financial problems. Taking in boarders at her home did not cover the expenses of raising three children.

That winter, Nabby gave birth to a daughter. She named her Caroline Amelia, and the excited Grandma Adams traveled to see her as soon as the weather permitted. She visited her son, Charles, too. He would soon marry Nabby's sister-in-law, Sally Smith. Abigail thought Sally would be good for Charles.

Jay's Treaty

In 1794, John Jay, a member of the Supreme Court, negotiated a treaty with England. War was averted, but the treaty was unpopular. Jay had made some concessions that people did not like. The treaty did not stop British ships from capturing American sailors and forcing them to join the British Navy. It also did not open British ports to American trade.

George Washington decided to retire when his second term ended in 1797. John knew he would have to decide whether to run for president in 1796. It was likely the Federalists would nominate him, and he was sure the Republicans would support Jefferson.

Abigail thought it was John's duty to run for president, although she knew it would be "a most unpleasant seat, full of thorns, briars, thistles . . ."[16]

In September, Washington had his farewell address to the country printed in the newspapers, instead of delivering it aloud. Abigail wrote, "All America is or ought to be in mourning . . . We shall not look upon his like again."[17]

The President's Wife

John Adams ran for the presidency against Thomas Jefferson, and on February 8, when the ballots were counted, Adams won by a narrow margin. He received seventy-one votes to Jefferson's sixty-eight votes. Under the system then being used, this meant that John Adams was president and Jefferson vice president. It was awkward to have members of opposing parties heading up the government together.

John Adams defeated Thomas Jefferson to win the presidency in 1796.

Abigail, responded to the news, writing to her husband, John: "My dearest friend . . . arm yourself with patience and forbearance and be not dismayed, and may God and the people support you. Having put your hand to the plow, you must not look back."[18]

10

FOUR YEARS AS FIRST LADY

On March 4, 1797, the morning of his inauguration, Abigail Adams wrote to John: "You have this day to declare yourself head of a nation. . . . My thoughts and my meditations are with you, though personally absent. . . . My feelings are not those of pride . . . upon the occasion."[1]

John regretted that none of his family was present for the ceremony, but Abigail was too busy caring for John's seriously ill mother. She was pleased that George Washington had stayed in Philadelphia to witness the inauguration before going home to Mount Vernon in Virginia.

John settled into the president's house and hired servants, but he had terrible difficulties. He finally wrote to Abigail in despair, "The times are critical and dangerous, and I must have you here to assist me. I can do nothing without you."[2]

John's mother died in April, and Abigail wrote to John, "I am ready and willing to follow my husband wherever he chooses."[3] She left for Philadelphia on April 27, taking Louisa Smith and several servants with her.

To the President's House

On the way, they stopped to see Nabby and her two-year-old daughter, Caroline. The little red-haired girl was Nabby's only joy in life. The two of them were alone on an isolated farm. William Smith was off on another journey, and the boys were with Abigail's sister, Elizabeth.

The next stop was in New York, to see her son Charles, his wife, Sally, and the new baby, who had been named Susanna Boylston after John's mother. They were doing well, and Abigail pronounced Sally "a discreet woman . . . quite different from many of the Family."[4]

The last leg of the journey, from New York to Philadelphia, was made very unpleasant by heavy rains. Abigail described the muddy road as being "like a ploughd field, in furroughs of 2 feet in deepth, and . . . very dangerous."[5]

John delighted her by driving twenty-five miles out from the city in a carriage to meet her. She got into his carriage, and they had a lovely dinner in Pennsylvania and spent the night there together. They reached Philadelphia at sunset, and he told her he felt a renewal of courage and hope, now that she was at his side.[6]

Life as First Lady

Back in Philadelphia, the only hours Abigail could call her own were from 5:00 A.M. to 8:00 A.M. "I keep up my old Habit of rising at an early hour," she said. "If I did not, I should have little comand of my Time."[7]

At 8:00, she ate breakfast with John and Louisa, then dealt with all the details of running the house. She planned menus and ordered food for the day. She dressed at 11:00, then received company from noon until 3:00. Then they ate an elaborate meal, often with thirty or forty distinguished guests. After dinner, Abigail went out in her carriage, shopping, visiting, or just enjoying the countryside.

As First Lady, she was expected to entertain government officials frequently. She once had the entire Senate and Cabinet, thirty-eight men, at their home for a meal. She also planned a series of dinners for the House of Representatives.

While she was First Lady, Abigail continued her habit of letter writing, especially to her sister Mary. Abigail sometimes sent her a letter she had received and asked her to have it printed in the Boston paper, hoping to counteract some of the "lies, falsehoods . . . and bitterness" directed at John's administration. She told Mary she could not get through a week without a letter from her.[8]

When Congress recessed in early July, the President and his wife went to Quincy for the summer. While there, they heard that John Quincy had married in London on July 26, 1797. Louisa Catherine Johnson's mother was British and her father American. Thomas Adams said she was sweet tempered and "a most lovely woman."[9] Abigail wrote to John Quincy, asking for a lock of Louisa's hair and a miniature portrait of her. She hoped they would become good friends.

More Worries for Abigail

Abigail was worried that Nabby's boys had learned bad habits from their father, so she had convinced Nabby to let them live with her sister, Elizabeth. When they visited

John Quincy Adams married Louisa Catherine Johnson in 1797. At first, there was some tension between Abigail and her new daughter-in-law, but they eventually became close friends.

Nabby on the way back to Philadelphia, Abigail begged her to bring Caroline and come with them, but Nabby did not want William to come home and find her gone.

Abigail worried about political issues, too. Many people at the time feared the United States would be drawn into a war with France, but some Federalists were actually hoping that would happen. In an effort to avoid war, John appointed three special envoys to negotiate with the French Directory, the group governing France. The Directory kept the envoys waiting for three weeks, then refused to see them. Three go-betweens, referred to as X, Y, and Z, said the representatives might be received if the United States paid them a bribe of $250,000.

The outrage made war seem inevitable. Congress strengthened the United States' military defense and created a Navy Department. Charles Maurice de Talleyrand, head of the French Directory, finally realized he was not going to get his way. He sent word that, if America sent a new minister, he would be received. Suddenly, John was a hero for ending the crisis without war. He and Abigail were cheered wherever they went, although some Federalists, who had wanted a war with France, were furious.

Problems With the Press

John's new popularity did not last long. Federalist policies were criticized viciously in the newspapers. One described the President as "old, querulous, bald, blind, crippled, toothless Adams."[10] Things got worse when John promoted his son John Quincy to the post of minister to Prussia.

Abigail thought the critical newspaper editors were "criminal."[11] She believed freedom of the press meant that newspapers had a responsibility to tell the truth. She thought public figures needed protection against lies and deliberate misrepresentations.

To silence critics of the government, Congress passed the Alien and Sedition Acts. These laws provided, among other things, for the arrest of newspaper editors who published statements against the government. Abigail was all in favor of these laws. She had argued for months that such laws were necessary. She thought they would protect her husband from attacks.

The laws were unpopular, especially among the Republicans at whom they were directed. By 1801, they had been repealed. However, they gave the Republicans a major issue to use against John Adams in the next election. Republicans said the Federalists were trying to silence the opposition and were willing to take away freedom of speech and freedom of the press.

An Unrestful Vacation

When Congress adjourned in July 1798, John and Abigail again headed home to Quincy. It was a hot, dusty journey home, and all along the way, they were met by well-wishers. Abigail said she would have preferred to "slide along . . . unnoticed and without parade."[12]

She became sick on the way home and was seriously ill by the time they got there. Boston doctors said she had a combination of dysentery, fever, and diabetes. They feared she might not survive. Louisa Smith and Nabby nursed her, and John would not leave her bedside. Gradually, her condition improved, but it was eleven weeks before she could even get out of bed.

Worry may have slowed her recuperation. She had not heard from Thomas, who was on his way home from Europe. She was afraid his ship had gone down. She also worried about Charles, who seemed emotionally unstable. He was drinking and could not account for money John Quincy had left with him to invest. And, as always, she worried about Nabby and her husband's inability to provide for his family.

John refused to return to Philadelphia until November, when Abigail was out of danger. She could not travel, so he took Louisa Smith and William Shaw with him. Louisa, now twenty-one, would act as his hostess, while William Shaw would serve as his secretary.

On his way south, John stopped to see Charles. Sally told John that Charles's drinking was causing him to neglect his law practice. Discouraged and depressed, John wrote to Abigail, "Happy Washington! Happy to be Childless! My Children give me more Pain than all my Enemies."[13]

Disagreeing, Abigail replied, "I do not consider GW at all a happier man because he has not children. If he has none to give him pain, he has none to give him pleasure."[14]

Thomas arrived in Philadelphia on January 10, 1799, just in time to attend the President's Tuesday night reception. John wept with joy when he saw his youngest son for the first time in almost five years.[15] When Thomas went to

Quincy to see his mother, she urged him to remain at home with her. He was determined to live on his own, however, and went to Philadelphia to resume his law practice.

Thomas had adopted the simple dress of the Quakers, members of the Society of Friends, a peace-loving religious group. He wore his hair short, instead of wearing a wig. John criticized his hairstyle. Soon after receiving his father's criticism, Thomas met a man who had known John years before. The man said John had once worn his hair the same way. "Did he, indeed, Sir?" Thomas answered. "The information is very acceptable to me and shall be not lost, for I have been somewhat persecuted since my return on account of the cut of my hair."[16]

That next summer, John returned to Quincy to be with Abigail, even though his friends in Congress advised him to stay in the capital. He supervised work on a new barn, and he and Abigail discussed an addition to the house.

Back to Political Life

Abigail felt well all summer, so she agreed to return to Philadelphia. This would be the last year the government was located there. John left in early October, stopping to see Nabby and Caroline on the way. William Smith had been offered a commission with the new army and was in New Jersey, helping to train the troops.

Sally, Charles Adams's wife, was now staying with Nabby. She did not know where Charles was. She told her father-in-law the sad story of her husband's decline. "I pitied her, I grieved, I mourned," reported John to Abigail. He knew he could do nothing to help his son, and he was angry and embarrassed.[17]

Nabby had agreed that she and Caroline would come to Philadelphia, so Abigail picked them up on her way. Sally and her girls were still with Nabby. Abigail was charmed with the little girls, Susan and Abbe.

Abigail, Nabby, and Caroline stopped to see Colonel Smith in New Jersey. "I acted . . . as your proxy [representative]," she told John, after reviewing the troops.[18]

Abigail was reunited with her son Thomas in Philadelphia. He would live with his parents in Philadelphia for the winter. She agreed to let him come and go as he liked.

Abigail was caught up in the social life of Philadelphia again. She described the latest styles to her sister Mary, saying cloaks of red broadcloth were "all the mode, trim'd with white furs."[19] However, Abigail did not care for many of the fashions. She thought some of the styles were indecent, with their low necklines and short sleeves. Well-dressed women were wearing their hair in curls and rouging their cheeks "Red as a Brick hearth."[20]

Political Problems, Personal Worries

Attention turned to the next presidential election. It seemed probable that John would lose his bid for a second term. Alexander Hamilton, secretary of the treasury, had spoken out against the peace commission John was sending to France. John and Abigail were being criticized unmercifully.

John's annual speech to Congress was well received. A few days later, on December 14, George Washington died. The actual funeral took place at Mount Vernon, in Virginia, but there was a mock funeral held in Philadelphia to honor the former president. The funeral procession passed along unpaved streets with mud so deep it sucked off some of the men's shoes. Abigail attended the service, which lasted from 11:00 until 4:00, then hurried home to preside at a formal dinner for thirty people.

In the spring of 1800, Gilbert Stuart painted Abigail's portrait. He said he wished he could have painted her when she was young. "I should have had a perfect Venus," he remarked.

"So he would," answered John.[21]

In May, Abigail left for Quincy, while John went to inspect the new "Federal City" being built on the banks of the Potomac. Stopping to see Nabby, Abigail learned that William Smith was again out of work. Nabby was depressed.

Charles had come home, but his condition was deteriorating fast. It broke Abigail's heart to see him this way. "Ruin and destruction have swallowed him up," she said.[22] She took his daughter, Susan, home with her to Quincy for the summer.

Work on the addition to the house was going well. Abigail moved her finest furniture from Europe and the family portraits into the huge drawing room, which was cool and bright.

John had a new study upstairs, and there was a much larger kitchen.

Nabby and Caroline spent the summer there, and John got home in July. Abigail wrote to John Quincy that he should resign his post in Europe and come home. She missed him and had not yet met his wife. If a Republican won the election for president, he would be recalled anyway, she reasoned. John Quincy gently told his mother it would be proper to wait to be recalled. He liked it in Europe and felt his presence there was important.

Washington, D.C.

John left by himself for the new capital. Abigail followed when Mary, who had been ill, was feeling better. On his first night in the new Executive Mansion, John wrote, "I pray Heaven to bestow the best of Blessings on this House and on all that shall hereafter inhabit it. May none but honest and wise Men ever rule under this roof!"[23]

Abigail stopped to see Charles, who was desperately ill and miserable at the home of a friend. Listening to his racking cough, she knew this was probably the last time she would see him alive.

She was somewhat cheered by a pleasant visit with Thomas in Philadelphia, then she set out for Washington. She had no trouble traveling between Philadelphia and Baltimore, but the last leg of the journey was a nightmare. They took a wrong turn, got lost in the woods, and wasted several hours. Finally they met an acquaintance, Major Snowden, who insisted that they stay at his estate. Abigail was relieved, although she hated to be a burden to anyone.

When she finally arrived in the capital city, Abigail was not impressed by Washington, the name chosen for the new capital city formerly called Federal City. Washington had only 109 permanent dwellings and the streets were muddy and unimproved. The President's House, which we now know as the White House, was a huge mansion on the banks of the Potomac. It was damp and cold and was not completely finished. There was little furniture and few servants.

Abigail tried to organize the household. She wrote to Nabby, "I patch up, but it is hard work." She told Nabby to "Keep all this to yourself," and said if anyone asked how her

Famous painter Gilbert Stuart painted this portrait of Abigail Adams. He expressed his sorrow that he could not capture the beauty she must have had in her younger years.

mother liked Washington, to tell them that "the situation is beautiful, which is true."[24]

Three weeks later, Charles Adams died at the age of thirty. His drinking had taken its toll. Abigail consoled herself by writing to Mary: "I know, my much loved Sister, that you will mingle in my sorrow and weep with me over the Grave of a poor unhappy child . . . He was beloved, in spight of his Errors, and all spoke with grief and sorrow for his habits."[25]

Abigail kept Charles's daughter Susan and brought her up as her own. After a few months with her parents, his widow, Sally, brought their other daughter, Abbe, and came to live with the Adamses.

Loss of the Presidency

Abigail did not have to live long in the unfinished President's House. John lost the presidential election of 1800 to Thomas Jefferson. It was a close race, and Abigail had mixed feelings. She wanted to retire to the farm but she knew John had been driven to serve his country. She wondered if he would be happy settling down at home.

Right after the election, news came that a peace treaty had been signed in Paris on October 30. Despite his failure to hold on to the presidency, John had been able to avoid a war with France over shipping and trade.

11

DOWN ON THE FARM— THE LATER YEARS

Now that Thomas Jefferson had been elected president, Abigail and John prepared to return to Quincy. Before leaving Washington, they invited Jefferson to dinner. They had political disagreements with the new president but were willing to ignore their differences and still enjoyed his company. Abigail was surprised and touched when Jefferson stopped to say good-bye to her before she and Louisa set out for Quincy in mid-February.

John spent his last few days in office appointing judges to some of the new courts. He appointed John Marshall Chief Justice of the Supreme Court, which was the one thing Jefferson thought was "personally unkind." He thought he should have been able to choose the new judges himself.[1]

John left Washington early on the morning of Jefferson's inauguration. He arrived home two weeks later,

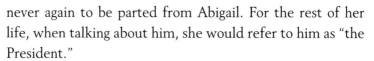

A Hard Trip Home
The Susquehanna River was not frozen solidly enough to hold them and the horses and carriage at one time. There was no bridge, so they sent one horse across at a time, then some men pushed the empty carriage across. Next, Abigail, Louisa, and the servants got into a boat on runners, and the men pushed them across. They just made it to the other side, and the men broke through the ice and were wet halfway to their knees.

never again to be parted from Abigail. For the rest of her life, when talking about him, she would refer to him as "the President."

Abigail wrote to thank William Smith for raspberry bushes and strawberry vines he had sent her. She also gave him a message for Nabby: "Tell her I have commenced my operation of dairywoman; and she might see me, at five o'clock in the morning skimming my milk."[2] She and John had long joked about her settling down to be a milkmaid.

Home Again

Abigail busied herself with her house, garden, and grandchildren. She kept up a steady correspondence with friends and relatives. She wrote to Thomas Adams, "You will find your father in his fields, attending to his hay-makers. The crops of hay have been abundant."[3]

In September, John Quincy, his wife, and their little boy arrived in Philadelphia. He brought Louisa and the baby to Quincy. John and Abigail were eager to meet her, but poor Louisa was so nervous, she found it impossible to

Just before leaving the presidency, John Adams appointed judges who he believed would support his political views, including John Marshall, who would become one of the most influential justices ever to sit on the Supreme Court.

relax. She came from a wealthy, powerful family and was used to a totally different way of life. She was very shy, and said later, "Had I steped into Noah's Ark i do not think I could have been more utterly astonished."[4]

Abigail and John's niece, Louisa Smith, now twenty-four, was unreasonably jealous of the new Louisa. She refused to eat and ran from the dinner table in tears.

Abigail interpreted Louisa's shyness as pride and thought she was a fine lady who would never fit in with their simple way of life. Abigail was kind to her, but Louisa felt inadequate. She thought the Adamses' manners were very stiff and formal. She wrote and told friends that "hanging and marriage were strongly assimilated."[5]

On the other hand, Louisa and John Adams liked each other immediately. "The Old Gentleman took a fancy to me," she said.[6]

Mother of a Promising Politician

John Quincy moved his family to a nearby farm and went back to his law practice in Boston. In 1803, at the age of thirty-six, he was elected senator from Massachusetts. Abigail had hoped he would not follow in his father's footsteps and get into politics, but she was proud of him. He and Louisa now had another little boy, John.

John Quincy wrote Abigail letters about politics, and Louisa wrote her mother-in-law about the social life in Washington. Abigail took care of their farm, as Mary Cranch and Cotton Tufts had taken care of her farm when she was away while her husband was serving the government.

Like his parents before him, John Quincy found that it was too expensive for his whole family to live in Washington. In 1805, they left the boys at the farm with Abigail and John, but Louisa missed them so much, she refused to be separated from them again.

One year, when Congress recessed, John Quincy went alone to stay with his parents, while Louisa took the boys to her parents' home in Washington. Louisa wrote, saying, "[Their son] George is very angry with you he says you are very naughty to go away and leave him."[7] Finally, Louisa agreed to stay in Quincy with the boys while John Quincy was in Washington, as Abigail had done.

Thomas Adams made his mother very happy in December 1803 when he came home to live. John Quincy advised Abigail to leave Thomas alone and not offer advice on "his mode of life and his pursuits."[8]

In 1805, Thomas married Ann Harrod, who was known affectionately as Nancy. They moved in with his parents, and Nancy and Abigail became the best of friends. Thomas became a judge, and they started their family.

That same summer, Nabby and the children visited. Abigail and John were happiest when surrounded by children. Grandpa John spoiled the grandchildren and played with them. Grandma Abigail felt responsible for their training and discipline, but she loved them as much as he did.

When William Smith took his boys home from Elizabeth's, Abigail was angry. "It is a pitty two such fine Boys should be in a way to be ruined," she said. "Their Father has no Head to plan out their education."[9]

In 1806, William Smith became involved in a scheme to free the people of Venezuela from the Spanish and ended up in jail. Unfortunately, he had also involved young William, then eighteen. Nabby went to live on the prison grounds to be near her husband. He was acquitted, but his involvement in the situation seemed to be another example of his instability.

Family and Friends

The next summer, in 1807, Abigail was again surrounded by family. She would always remember the last Sunday before John Quincy left for Washington to serve in the Senate. All her living children and all but one of her grandchildren were there. Only John Smith, Nabby's son, was missing.

William Smith acquired a farm in Lebanon, New York. Abigail was determined to have Nabby and Caroline stay with her through the winter. William, however, was just as determined, and he came to Quincy to get his family. Abigail was learning that she could not always run the lives of her children and grandchildren to suit herself.

When James Madison took the office of president in 1809, he nominated John Quincy as ambassador to Russia. John Quincy promptly accepted, and Abigail sadly said good-bye again. His sons George and John stayed behind to live with their grandparents. John Quincy and Louisa took with them baby Charles and Nabby's son William, who would serve as John Quincy's private secretary on the mission.

In 1811, the Adams family faced more than its share of sickness. Mary Cranch, Abigail's sister, was suffering from consumption, a serious lung disease. She was not expected to live. Then word came that Nabby had found a tumor in her breast. Abigail insisted she come to Boston for medical advice. Nabby finally came, bringing John and Caroline with her. Nabby wrote to Dr. Benjamin Rush, her father's dear friend in Philadelphia. From the symptoms she described, Dr. Rush concluded that immediate surgery was her only chance of survival.[10]

Nabby was terrified of the pain, since there was no anesthesia available in those days. But she had the breast removed in early October, in a twenty-five-minute surgery. It took an hour to dress the wound, but the doctors said she was cured. She stayed with her parents for several months. It was a long time before she could use her arm to eat or dress herself.

A few days after Nabby's surgery, Mary's husband, Richard Cranch, died of a stroke. Left without him, Mary, who had barely been hanging on to life, gave up. She died in her sleep the next day.

This double blow, coming on top of Nabby's medical problems, was very hard on Abigail. "The threefold silken cord [the way she referred to the relationships of the three sisters] is broken," she told her sister Elizabeth.[11] Unable to deal with the stress, Abigail fell ill in August. She sent George and John to Elizabeth's home. She just did not have the strength to care for them.

The War of 1812

In 1812, James Madison, who had become president in 1809, was reelected, and the War of 1812 broke out with England. Freedom of the seas was the main issue. The

British were stopping American ships and forcing the sailors to join their navy. They also stirred up trouble with the American Indians on the western frontier.[12]

From the upstairs windows of the house in Quincy, Abigail could see British cruisers patrolling the New England coast. The scary sight must have reminded her of the days during the American Revolution when she could see British ships in Boston Harbor.

Thomas's baby daughter died that year, in the same room where her grandfather, John Adams, had been born. John Adams mourned her death, asking, "Why was I preserved three quarters of a century, and that rose cropped in the bud?"[13]

More bad news soon came from Russia. Louisa and John Quincy's little daughter had died at the age of thirteen months. He said the little girl had been "our only daughter, and lovely as a Seraph [angel] upon the earth."[14]

Renewing Old Friendships

Abigail wrote to Louisa of her own grief forty years earlier when baby Suky had died. This was the first time she had been able to talk about that loss, and it drew her and Louisa closer together.

Soon after, Abigail reconciled with Mercy Warren, her old friend from revolutionary days. Their friendship had ended in 1805 when Mercy published a book, *History of the Revolution*. In it, she had criticized John Adams and his presidential policies, which made John and Abigail furious.

Abigail now felt an urge to make up with her old friend. She wrote to Mercy, who was now eighty years old. Mercy was delighted, and their correspondence flourished once again. In 1812, Abigail visited her for the first time in years.

It was also time to make amends with Thomas Jefferson. Eight years earlier, Abigail had written a letter of condolence when his daughter died. They had exchanged several letters, but their political differences proved too strong to allow their friendship to survive. Their mutual friend Dr. Benjamin Rush appealed to both Jefferson and John Adams to reconcile their differences. John Adams made the first move, and Jefferson answered right away. Both men agreed to disagree. They would let future generations decide who was right. They proceeded to exchange rich, wonderful letters.

Painful Good-byes

In the spring of 1813, Nabby was sick with what she thought was rheumatism. Actually, it was a recurrence of her cancer. By June of that year, she was so sick she could barely walk. Abigail was afraid she would never see her daughter again. Nabby was too sick to travel, and Abigail was too old to make the three-hundred-mile trip to Lebanon.

Nabby knew she was dying, and she wanted to see her parents one more time. She, John, and Caroline made the trip in a bumpy carriage. They arrived at the end of July, and she was carried into the house and made comfortable. Two weeks later, her husband came from Washington. He had been elected to Congress and was attending the session. Abigail, Susan, Caroline, and Louisa Smith did everything they could for Nabby, but she died on August 15.

Abigail was devastated. She was closer to this daughter than to any of her other children. She wrote to John Quincy, "The wound which has lacerated my Bosom cannot be healed."[15] Her one consolation was that Caroline, who had always been one of her favorite grandchildren, continued to live with her until her marriage two years later.

Although she was sick a lot, nothing seemed to slow Abigail down. John told John Quincy, "Your Mother . . . must take upon herself the Duties of Granddaughter, Niece, Maids, Husband and all. She must be allways writing to you and all her Grand children."[16]

Abigail herself said, "I would rather have too much [to do] than too little. Life stagnates without action. I could never bear to merely vegetate."[17]

Many close friends and relatives were dying—Benjamin Rush, Mercy Warren, and Elbridge Gerry, Abigail's correspondent in Congress while John was abroad. Then, in April 1815, Abigail's sister Elizabeth died suddenly. Abigail wondered why she, the older sister, was still living. She decided it was time to make a will. She tried to be "even-handed" with her two sons. She left money, jewelry, and clothing to her nieces and granddaughters. She complained that her hair was "frosted," her eyesight failing, and her memory like a "sieve."[18]

The week after Elizabeth died, Abigail put John Quincy's sons George and John on a ship bound for England. John Quincy had been named minister to the Court of St. James, as his father had been before him. He had recently helped negotiate the Treaty of Ghent, which ended the War of 1812.

At the end of that year, Abigail's dear uncle Cotton Tufts died. He had taken care of their finances when they were abroad, advised them about money, and helped Abigail whenever John was away. Truly Uncle Tufts had been their "most ancient, venerable, and most beloved friend."[19]

Then William Smith died, with Caroline at his bedside. Trying to be charitable, John wrote to John Quincy, "Be to his virtues ever kind, to his faults a little blind. The world will never know all the good or all the evil he has done."[20]

By 1816, John and Abigail were alone in the big house, except for Louisa Smith, who was like a real daughter to them. They were often lonely, missing their children, who were busy leading their own lives.

In November 1816, John Quincy was appointed secretary of state by the new president, James Monroe. Fearing he would refuse and she might never see him again, Abigail wrote to him, "The voice of the nation calls you home. The government calls you home—and your parents unite in the call. To this summons you must not, you cannot refuse your assent."[21]

John Quincy's ship docked in New York on August 6, 1817, after he had spent almost eight years in Europe. Two weeks later, he arrived in Quincy, and young John threw himself into his grandmother's arms, as sixteen-year-old George cried, "O, Grandmother! O Grandmother!"[22] It was Charles's tenth birthday, but he had been in Europe so long, he did not remember his grandparents.

Death of a Great Lady

In October 1818, Abigail came down with typhoid fever. Lucy Cranch Greenleaf, Mary's daughter, came to help Louisa Smith take care of her. John Adams stayed constantly by her bedside.

Suddenly, on October 28, she seemed to lose her strength. She told John she knew she was dying. She turned to Lucy and said she had been "a mother to me," then closed her eyes and went to sleep.[23] She was almost seventy-four. She died without pain and with her wits still sharp.

John looked down at her and said, "I wish I could lay down beside her and die too."[24]

THE LEGACY OF ABIGAIL ADAMS

I n a time when women's opinions were largely discounted, Abigail Adams had a real influence on the course of politics in the United States. Throughout her husband's career, she remained his confidante and most trusted advisor. Although they agreed on most political questions, her opinions were often more extreme than his, and she did not hesitate to voice them.

Abigail has sometimes been called the first feminist in America. She does not completely fit the role of feminist as we define it today. She always believed that a woman's most important roles in life were those of wife and mother. However, she did not think a woman needed to be limited by these roles.

In her famous "Remember the Ladies" letter to John Adams in 1776, she made it clear that husbands should not have total control over their wives. She noted that "All men would be tyrants if they could."[1] John did not agree with her. He accepted her as his equal in everything but did not believe most women were as capable as his extraordinary wife.

Abigail Adams did not advocate that women vote or hold office, but she had a strong interest in politics. She and her sisters grew up in a home where politics was the main topic of conversation with visitors. She came to resent the disruption politics made in her family life, but when she could be with John, she enjoyed being a political wife.

Abigail never got over her feeling that her education had been inadequate. She was one of the best-educated women in America at the time, but she was mainly self-educated through her reading. She knew that in order to be free from the "tyranny" of men, women would have to be educated. She made sure that her daughter, Nabby, learned Latin, which was very unusual for a girl at that time. Abigail wrote to John in 1778, "in this country, you need not be told how much female education is neglected, nor how fashionable it has been to ridicule female learning; though I acknowledge it my happiness to be connected with a person of a more generous mind and liberal sentiments."[2] Abigail's interest in books and learning had been one of the things that first attracted John to her.

Abigail Adams was a strong woman who cared a great deal for family. Her two sisters were her closest friends throughout her life, and she was generous with them and their children. Frequently, she helped them out with small sums of money and gifts of clothing and books.

She brought up her own four children, as well as a niece and several grandchildren. She also had great influence on her other nieces, nephews, and grandchildren. She was the one who held the Adams family together. Her daughter-in-law, Louisa Adams, said after Abigail's death that her mother-in-law had been "the guiding planet around which all revolved."[3]

Although Abigail was a good mother, she did have a tendency to try to run the lives of her children and grandchildren. Of the Adamses' four children, Nabby was the one most intimidated by her mother. She felt that others expected her to be like Abigail, and she was very different in personality and ability. Apparently, she felt her mother expected too much of her, and she often withdrew into herself, becoming depressed.[4] Marriage to William Smith, with his irresponsible behavior, did nothing to help her feelings of inadequacy.

The Adams boys were more likely to stand up to their mother, or ignore her attempts at manipulation. She tried many times to get Thomas to move back home, but he did so only when he was ready. She wrote to John Quincy and tried to convince him to come home from Europe in 1800, but he resisted her efforts. However, he did not resent her. When she died, he wrote in his diary, "Life is no longer to

John Quincy Adams as President
Abigail Adams did not live to see her son become president, although her husband did. John Quincy was elected in 1824, making Abigail the only woman—until Barbara Bush in 2001—to be both the wife and the mother of a president.

Abigail Adams was not only a First Lady, but she was also the mother of another president, John Quincy Adams.

me what it was. My home is no longer the abode of my mother."[5]

The most important legacy Abigail Adams left was her letters. More than two thousand of them survive. They give us a wonderful picture of her, her family, and her times. John realized before he went to the First Continental Congress that their letters might be important to future generations. He told her "to put them up safe and preserve them. They may exhibit to our posterity a kind of picture of the manners, opinions, and principles of these times of perplexity, danger, and distress."[6]

Abigail's life with John was a love affair that never ended. Their love for one another grew deeper as the years went on, despite the fact that they were often apart for long periods of time. Abigail Adams was a great influence on her family, her country, and those who would come after her.

At her funeral, Samuel Kirkland, president of Harvard, said, "[she] was a minister of blessings to all within her influence . . . she received the good of her existence with a cheerful and grateful heart . . . she bore adversity with an equal mind."[7]

CHRONOLOGY

1744—Born in Weymouth, Massachusetts, on November 22.

1764—Marries John Adams on October 25.

1765—Abigail Adams (Nabby) born on July 14.

1767—John Quincy Adams born on July 11.

1768—Susanna Adams born on December 28.

1770—Susanna Adams dies on February 6; Boston Massacre occurs; Charles Adams born on May 29.

1772—Thomas Boylston Adams born on September 15.

1773—Boston Tea Party.

1774—First Continental Congress meets in Philadelphia with John Adams as a delegate.

1775—Revolutionary War begins with the Battles of Lexington and Concord.

1776—Declaration of Independence adopted by colonies.

1777—Abigail has still-born baby girl, Elizabeth, on July 11.

1778—John and John Quincy go to France, where John is to help negotiate a treaty; Louisa Smith, Abigail's two-year-old niece, moves in with the family.

1779—John and John Quincy return from Europe; John goes back to Europe, taking both John Quincy and Charles.

1781—Cornwallis surrenders at Yorktown in the last battle of the Revolution.

1784—Abigail and Nabby sail to Europe.

1785—John is appointed first American ambassador to the Court of St. James in London.

1786—Nabby marries Colonel William S. Smith on June 12.

1788—Abigail and John return from Europe.

1789—John is elected vice president.

1792—Washington and Adams are reelected as president and vice president.

1795—Charles marries Sally Smith.

1797—John is elected president; John Quincy marries Louisa Catherine Johnson in Europe.

1798—The Alien and Sedition Acts are passed.

1800—Washington, D.C., becomes the nation's capital.

1801—Thomas Jefferson defeats John Adams in the presidential election.

1805—Thomas marries Ann Harrod.

1809—John Quincy is appointed ambassador to Russia.

1811—Nabby discovers she has breast cancer and undergoes a mastectomy.

1812—War breaks out with England.

1813—Nabby dies from cancer.

1817—John Quincy becomes secretary of state.

1818—Abigail dies on October 28 in Quincy, Massachusetts.

CHAPTER NOTES

Chapter 1. The War Begins

1. Nagel, Paul C., *John Quincy Adams* (New York: Alfred A. Knopf, 1997), p. 8.

2. *World Book Encyclopedia* (Chicago: Field Enterprises Educational Corporation, 1962), vol. 14, p. 675.

3. L. H. Butterfield, ed., *The Book of Abigail and John: Selected Letters of the Adams Family, 1762–1784* (Cambridge, Mass.: Harvard University Press, 1975), p. 89.

4. Charles Francis Adams, ed., *Memoirs of John Quincy Adams* (Philadelphia: J.B. Lippincott and Co., 1874), p. 545.

5. Dorothie Bobbe, *Abigail Adams: The Second First Lady* (New York: Minton, Balch, & Company, 1929), p. 70.

Chapter 2. The Preacher's Daughter Grows Up

1. John Ferling, *John Adams: A Life* (Knoxville, TN: The University of Tennessee Press, 1992), p. 31.

2. Lynne Withey, *Dearest Friend: A Life of Abigail Adams* (New York: The Free Press, 1981), p. 6.

3. Ibid., p. 4.

4. Natalie S. Bober, *Abigail Adams: Witness to a Revolution* (New York: Atheneum, 1995), p. 57.

5. Withey, p. 6.

6. Catherine Drinker Bowen, *John Adams and the American Revolution* (Boston: Little, Brown, and Company, 1950), p. 235.

7. Paul C. Nagel, *The Adams Women* (New York: Oxford University Press, 1987), p. 12.

8. Laura E. Richards, *Abigail Adams and Her Times* (New York: D. Appleton and Company, 1917), pp. 12–13.

9. Withey, p. 11.

10. Richards, p. 16.

Chapter 3. Love and Marriage

1. L. H. Butterfield, ed., *The Book of Abigail and John: Selected Letters of the Adams Family, 1762–1784* (Cambridge, Mass: Harvard University Press, 1975), p. 17.

2. David McCullough, *John Adams* (New York: Simon & Schuster, 2001), p. 18.

3. Lynne Withey, *Dearest Friend: A Life of Abigail Adams* (New York: The Free Press, 1981), p. 14.

4. Butterfield, p. 17.

5. Ibid., p. 42.

6. Ibid., p. 43.

7. Ibid., p. 40.

8. Ibid., p. 39.

9. Withey, p. 31.

10. Butterfield, p. 39.

11. Ibid., p. 45.

Chapter 4. Unrest in the Colonies

1. Lynne Withey, *Dearest Friend: A Life of Abigail Adams* (New York: The Free Press, 1981), p. 26.

2. Bancroft, George, *History of the United States* (New York: D. Appleton and Co., 1897), Vol. 3, p. 77.

3. John Adams, *Diary and Autobiography of John Adams* (Cambridge, Mass.: Belknap Press of Harvard University, 1962), p. 265.

4. L. H. Butterfield, *Adams Family Correspondence* (Cambridge, Mass: Belknap Press of Harvard University, 1963), p. 53.

5. Withey, p. 40.

6. Butterfield, p. 62.

7. Withey, p. 40.

8. David McCullough, *John Adams* (New York: Simon & Schuster, 2001), p. 69.

9. L. H. Butterfield, ed., *The Book of Abigail and John: Selected Letters of the Adams Family, 1762–1784* (Cambridge, Mass: Harvard University Press, 1975), p. 49.

10. Withey, p. 42.

11. John Ferling, *John Adams: A Life* (Knoxville, TN: The University of Tennessee Press, 1992), pp. 91–92.

12. Natalie S. Bober, *Abigail Adams: Witness to a Revolution* (New York: Atheneum, 1995), p. 44.

13. Butterfield, *The Book of Abigail and John*, p. 53.

14. Bober, p. 47.

Chapter 5. Early Years of the Revolution

1. Samuel McCoy, *This Man Adams* (New York), Brentano's, 1928), p. 163.

2. Lynne Withey, *Dearest Friend: A Life of Abigail Adams* (New York: The Free Press, 1981), p. 89.

3. Laura E. Richards, *Abigail Adams and Her Times* (New York: D. Appleton and Company, 1917), p. 130.

4. Ibid., p. 89.

5. L. H. Butterfield, ed., *The Book of Abigail and John: Selected Letters of the Adams Family, 1762–1784* (Cambridge, Mass.: Harvard University Press, 1975), p. 95.

6. Ibid., p. 100.

7. Richards, p. 96.

8. L. H. Butterfield, *Adams Family Correspondence* (Cambridge, Mass.: Belknap Press of Harvard University Press, 1963), pp. 309–310.

9. Butterfield, *The Book of Abigail and John*, p. 76.

10. Ibid., p. 107.

11. Butterfield, *Adams Family Correspondence*, p. 310.

12. Butterfield, *Book of Abigail and John*, p. 108.

13. Ibid., p. 156.

14. Richards, p. 156.

15. Ibid., pp. 2–5.

16. Withey, p. 84.

17. Butterfield, *Book of Abigail and John*, p. 180.

18. Ibid., p. 181.

19. Withey, p. 91.

20. Butterfield, *Book of Abigail and John*, p. 87.

Chapter 6. Home Alone

1. Natalie S. Bober, *Abigail Adams: Witness to a Revolution* (New York: Atheneum, 1995), p. 91.

2. Lynne Withey, *Dearest Friend: A Life of Abigail Adams* (New York: The Free Press, 1981), p. 100.

3. Dorothie Bobbe, *Abigail Adams: The Second First Lady* (New York: Minton, Balch and Company, 1929), p. 174.

4. Laura E. Richards, *Abigail Adams and Her Times* (New York: D. Appleton and Company, 1917), p. 169.

5. Bobbe, p. 216.

6. Withey, pp. 105–106.

7. Ibid., p. 109.

8. Ibid., p. 110.

9. L. H. Butterfield, ed., *The Book of Abigail and John: Selected Letters of the Adams Family, 1762–1784* (Cambridge, Mass.: Harvard University Press, 1975), pp. 232–233.

10. Paul C. Nagel, *John Quincy Adams* (New York: Alfred A. Knopf, 1997), p. 17.

Chapter 7. Alone Again

1. L.H. Butterfield, ed., *Adams Family Correspondence* (Cambridge, Mass.: Belknap Press of Harvard University Press, 1963), pp. 244–245.

2. Ibid., pp. 257–259.

3. Ibid., pp. 302–303.

4. Lynne Withey, *Dearest Friend: A Life of Abigail Adams* (New York: The Free Press, 1981), p. 133.

5. David McCullough, *John Adams* (New York: Simon & Schuster, 2001), p. 288.

6. L. H. Butterfield, ed., *The Book of Abigail and John: Selected Letters of the Adams Family, 1762–1784* (Cambridge, Mass.: Harvard University Press, 1975), p. 338.

7. McCullough, p. 289.

8. Butterfield, *The Book of Abigail and John*, p. 363.

Chapter 8. Abigail Goes to Europe

1. L. H. Butterfield, ed., *The Book of Abigail and John: Selected Letters of the Adams Family, 1762–1784* (Cambridge, Mass.: Harvard University Press, 1975), p. 380.

2. Laura E. Richards, *Abigail Adams and Her Times* (New York: D. Appleton and Company, 1917), p. 200.

3. Anna Husted Burleigh, *John Adams* (New Rochelle, NY: Arlington House, 1969), p. 385.

4. Butterfield, p. 385.

5. Richards, p. 204.

6. Butterfield, p. 388.

7. Lynne Withey, *Dearest Friend: A Life of Abigail Adams* (New York: The Free Press, 1981), p. 158.

8. Dorothie Bobbe, *Abigail Adams: The Second First Lady* (New York: Minton, Balch and Company, 1929), p. 226.

9. Natalie S. Bober, *Abigail Adams: Witness to a Revolution* (New York: Atheneum, 1995), p. 127.

10. Bobbe, p. 227.

11. Butterfield, p. 395.

12. Withey, p. 160.

13. Ibid.

14. Richards, p. 208.

15. Withey, p. 164.

16. John Ferling, *John Adams: A Life* (Knoxville, TN: The University of Tennessee Press, 1992), p. 273.

17. Richards, p. 213.

18. David McCullough, *John Adams* (New York: Simon & Schuster, 2001), p. 338.

19. Bober, p. 137.

20. Withey, p. 176.

21. Richards, p. 219.

22. Bober, p. 140.

23. McCullough, p. 362.

24. Withey, p. 190.

25. Ibid., p. 191.

26. McCullough, p. 365.

27. Bober, p. 144.

28. Ibid., p. 146.

29. McCullough, p. 371.

30. Bober, p. 151.

31. Paul M. Zall, *Founding Mothers: Profiles of Ten Wives of America's Founding Fathers* (Bowie, Md.: Heritage Books, 1991), p. 52.

32. Bober, p. 152.

Chapter 9. The Vice President's Wife

1. Lynne Withey, *Dearest Friend: A Life of Abigail Adams* (New York: The Free Press, 1981), p. 204.

2. David McCullough, *John Adams* (New York: Simon & Schuster, 2001), p. 391.

3. Withey, p. 203.

4. Ibid., p. 206.

5. Ibid, p. 232.

6. Bober, p. 167.

7. Ibid., p. 163.

8. Withey, p. 216.

9. Laura E. Richards, *Abigail Adams and Her Times* (New York: D. Appleton and Company, 1917), p. 240.

10. Bober, p. 167.

11. Withey, p. 220.

12. Richards, p. 241.

13. Withey, p. 225.

14. McCullough, p. 441.

15. Withey, p. 232.

16. Bober, p. 177.

17. Ibid.

18. Withey, p. 240.

Chapter 10. Four Years as First Lady

1. Laura E. Richards, *Abigail Adams and Her Times* (New York: D. Appleton and Company, 1917), pp. 246–247.

2. David McCullough, *John Adams* (New York: Simon & Schuster, 2001), p. 479.

3. Natalie S. Bober, *Abigail Adams: Witness to a Revolution* (New York: Atheneum, 1995), p. 181.

4. Lynne Withey, *Dearest Friend: A Life of Abigail Adams* (New York: The Free Press, 1981), p. 248.

5. Ibid.

6. Bober, p. 183.

7. Withey, p. 249.

8. Bober, p. 183.

9. Ibid., p. 184.

10. McCullough, p. 500.

11. Bober, p. 188.

12. Ibid., p. 189.

13. John Ferling, *John Adams: A Life* (Knoxville, TN: The University of Tennessee Press, 1992), p. 388.

14. Ibid.

15. Bober, p. 191.

16. Withey, p. 262.

17. McCullough, p. 529.

18. Bober, p. 193.

19. Ibid.

20. Ibid.

21. McCullough, p. 545.

22. Ibid., p. 548.

23. Ibid., p. 551.

24. Richards, p. 252.

25. Bober, p. 198.

Chapter 11. Down on the Farm—The later Years.

1. Natalie S. Bober, *Abigail Adams: Witness to a Revolution* (New York: Atheneum, 1995), p. 202.

2. Laura E. Richards, *Abigail Adams and Her Times* (New York: D. Appleton and Company, 1917), p. 26.

3. Ibid.

4. David McCullough, *John Adams* (New York: Simon & Schuster, 2001), p. 574.

5. Margaret Truman, *First Ladies* (New York: Random House, 1995), p. 279.

6. Ibid.

7. Lynne Withey, *Dearest Friend: A Life of Abigail Adams* (New York: The Free Press, 1981), p. 290.

8. Ibid., p. 289.

9. Ibid., p. 281.

10. McCullough, p. 602.

11. Richard T. Current, *American History: A Survey* (New York: Alfred A. Knopf, 1987), pp. 214–218.

12. Ibid., pp. 214–220.

13. McCullough, p. 609.

14. Paul C. Nagel, *John Quincy Adams* (New York: Alfred A. Knopf, 1997), p. 209.

15. Withey, p. 309.

16. Bober, p. 216.

17. Ibid., p. 215.

18. Ibid., p. 218.

19. Ibid.

20. Ibid., p. 219.

21. Withey, p. 310.

22. McCullough, p. 621.

23. Bober, p. 220.

24. McCullough, p. 623.

Chapter 12. The Legacy of Abigail Adams

1. David McCullough, *John Adams* (New York: Simon & Schuster, 2001), p. 104.

2. Susan Provost Beller, *Woman of Independence: The Life of Abigail Adams* (White Hall, Va.: Shoe Tree Press, 1992), p. 121.

3. Paul C. Nagel, *Adams Women* (New York: Oxford University Press, 1987), p. 158.

4. Ibid., pp. 99-101.

5. Milton Lomask, *John Quincy Adams: Son of the American Revolution* (New York: Farrar, Straus and Giroux, 1965), p. 86.

6. Natalie S. Bober, *Abigail Adams: Witness to a Revolution* (New York: Atheneum, 1995), p. 48.

7. Laura E. Richards, *Abigail Adams and Her Times* (New York: D. Appleton and Company, 1917), p. 280.

GLOSSARY

Alien and Sedition Acts—The Alien Act made it harder for foreigners to become citizens, while the Sedition Act punished those who spoke against the government.

alliance—An agreement between nations.

Articles of Confederation—The first governing document of the United States. It provided for a loose alliance among the separate states.

artillery—Heavy mounted guns, such as cannons.

Bill of Rights—The first ten amendments to the Constitution, which guarantee American citizens certain basic rights.

Boston Massacre—A scuffle in 1770 between colonists and British troops.

Boston Tea Party—A protest against the British tax on tea. Patriots dumped three shiploads of tea into Boston Harbor, rather than pay tax on it.

Cabinet—A group of official advisors to the president of the United States.

circuit court—A court that held sessions in various locations.

Constitution—Official plan of government for the United States.

Continental Congress—A group of representatives of the colonies that served as a governing body just before and during the Revolutionary War.

Declaration of Independence—A formal statement declaring America free of Great Britain.

Democratic-Republicans—Early political party that was against strong central government.

Directory—Group that governed France in the late 1790s.

Federalists—Early political party that believed in strong central government.

inoculation—Being injected with mild germs of a disease in order to build up resistance.

militia—An army made up of volunteer citizens and called in an emergency.

miniature—A very small painting, usually a portrait.

minister plenipotentiary—A diplomatic agent with full authority to act for the government.

patriot—One who is loyal to his country.

Quaker—A member of the Society of Friends, a peace-loving religious group.

Shays' Rebellion—A 1786 rebellion in Massachusetts, protesting taxes on land, among other things.

smallpox—A very contagious virus, similar to chickenpox but much more serious. Symptoms include chills, fever, and breaking out with spots.

XYZ Affair—An attempt by French officials to secure money from the United States in exchange for meeting with American diplomats.

FURTHER READING

Books

Akers, Charles W. *Abigail Adams: An American Woman.* Boston: Little, Brown and Company, 1980.

Bober, Natalie S. *Abigail Adams: Witness to a Revolution.* New York: Atheneum, 1995.

Butterfield, L. H., ed. *The Book of Abigail and John: Selected Letters of the Adams Family, 1762-1784.* Cambridge, Mass.: Harvard University Press, 1975.

Gelles, Edith B. *Portia: The World of Abigail Adams.* Bloomington: Indiana University Press, 1992.

Levin, Phyllis Lee. *Abigail Adams, A Biography.* New York: St. Martin's Press, 1987.

Nagel, Paul C. *The Adams Women.* New York: Oxford University Press, 1987.

Osborne, Angela. *Abigail Adams.* New York: Chelsea House Publishers, 1989.

Internet Addresses

Abigail Adams Birthplace. <http://southshoreserver.com/ abigailadams/>

Adams National Historic Site. <http://www.nps.gov/ adam>

National Women's Hall of Fame. <http://www.greatwomen. org/profile.php?id=5>

INDEX